RORY
MCILROY
THE BIOGRAPHY

RORY
MCILROY
THE BIOGRAPHY

FRANK WORRALL

JOHN BLAKE

Published by John Blake Publishing Ltd,
3 Bramber Court, 2 Bramber Road,
London W14 9PB, England

www.johnblakepublishing.co.uk

www.facebook.com/Johnblakepub facebook
twitter.com/johnblakepub twitter

First published in paperback in 2011
This edition published in 2013

ISBN: 978-1-78219-430-9

British Library Cataloguing-in-Publication Data:

A catalogue record for this book is available from the British Library.

Design by www.envydesign.co.uk

Printed in Great Britain by CPI Group (UK) Ltd, Croydon, CR0 4YY

1 3 5 7 9 10 8 6 4 2

Papers used by John Blake Publishing are natural, recyclable products made
from wood grown in sustainable forests. The manufacturing processes conform
to the environmental regulations of the country of origin.

Every attempt has been made to contact the relevant copyright-holders,
but some were unobtainable. We would be grateful if the
appropriate people could contact us.

This book is dedicated to Adrian Baker
of the *Mail on Sunday*

CONTENTS

ACKNOWLEDGEMENTS

Special thanks: John Blake, Allie Collins and all at John Blake Publishing. Andy Bucklow, the *Mail on Sunday*; Alan Feltham and the boys at *SunSport*, Bruce Waddell, the *Daily Record*, and Dominic Turnbull, the *Mail on Sunday*.

Thanks to: Danny Bottono, Lee Clayton, Steven Gordon, Dave Morgan, David and Nicki Burgess, Pravina Patel, Martin Creasy, Tim Smith, Derek Whitfield, David Michael, Alex Butler, Gary Edwards, Ian Rondeau, Colin Forshaw, John Fitzpatrick, Roy Stone, Tom Henderson Smith and Meg Graham.

Not forgetting: Angela, Frankie, Jude, Nat, Barbara, Frank, Bob and Stephen, Gill, Lucy, Alex, Suzanne, Michael and William.

INTRODUCTION

He is the boy who became a man in the space of three breathtaking months of 2011; the boy who broke under the pressure of The Masters in April of that year, yet who in June would conjure up one of the greatest all-time wins of the US Open. Proving that, yes, it's perfectly possible to triumph over adversity if you want it badly enough, if you persevere and refuse to give in, refuse to be beaten – especially after a very public humbling at Augusta.

And as Rory McIlroy held aloft the gleaming silver winner's trophy at Congressional that glorious early summer's day he gave the sport of golf the boost it so badly needed after the dark days of Tiger Woods' downfall. He propelled it back onto the front and the back pages for all the right reasons rather than those linked to a depressing downfall of excess and addiction.

At the same time, he opened up the game to a whole new generation – a group of kids who now wanted to be Rory McIlroy, who would head to the greens of local parks and clubs with their parents and embrace golf with a fresh enthusiasm. It was a remarkable double achievement for a young man of 21, who, at least as far as the non-golfing public were concerned, had seemingly come out of nowhere.

Rory's story is a phenomenal one, and it is also the story of a phenomenon: it's the tale of a boy from a country in which you need to be tough to survive let alone thrive, who beat all the odds to become the world's greatest golfer. This is the boy who refused to be defined by the Sectarian disputes that have so bedevilled his Northern Irish homeland over the years, the boy who insists he will not be dragged down by divides, whether Catholic or Protestant, British or Irish. One of a new generation eager for peace to conquer all, he is, in short, a fantastic advertisement for his country as well as his sport.

This is the story of a boy who, with the help of his wonderfully supportive parents, became a golfing prodigy – crawling around greens at 18 months, putting golf balls into washing machines and driving 40 yards by the age of five – and winning a World Championship for juniors at 10 years old.

By the age of 16 he had set a new course record at the demanding Royal Portrush and at 17, was ranked World Amateur No. 1 of 2007. Later that year he turned professional and soon established himself on the European Tour. He had his first win on the Tour in 2009, and on the

PGA Tour in 2010. Following this, he represented Europe in the 2010 Ryder Cup.

Then came the meltdown and the redemption. On 21 April 2011, he blew his chances of winning the US Masters at Augusta after establishing what seemed an unassailable lead during the first three days of play. Then, on 19 June 2011, he won the US Open, his first Major. But he didn't just win it – he secured it by annihilating the field, finishing with a record score of 16-under-par on his way to an eight-shot victory – and at 21, he was the youngest winner since Bobby Jones in 1923.

That wasn't the only record, though, as he won by eight shots over Jason Day. Rory's 72-hole aggregate score of 268 became the new US Open record – beating the previous peak of 272 held by Jack Nicklaus (Baltusrol, 1980), Lee Janzen (Baltusrol, 1993), Tiger Woods (Pebble Beach, 2000) and Jim Furyk (Olympia Fields, 2003). The 16-under-par beat Tiger Woods' 12-under at Pebble Beach Golf Links in 2000.

Now the talk was of Rory as the new Tiger Woods – the man who would claim the fallen hero's crown. There were similarities for sure but already Rory seemed more grounded and balanced an individual than Tiger ever had. Indeed, my opinion is that his meteoric rise is more on a par with that of another prodigy in a completely different sport.

In 2007, I wrote the first biography on a boy who was making a name for himself in the world of motor racing: Formula One newcomer Lewis Hamilton. With hindsight, I can see some very real similarities between Lewis and Rory.

Both came from backgrounds where the father sacrificed hours and effort to ensure his boy came through; both sweated in several jobs and travelled long distances to support their child. In the same way, both boys knew from an early age what they wanted to be, and how they would get there.

As a youngster Lewis was into karting, while Rory wanted nothing but a golf club and some balls. Both entered competitions from a young age and proved themselves to be top-notch and worthy of all the effort and sacrifice. In fact, both won early on and continued to progress and impress, moving forward with the help of a single, steady organisation – Lewis with McLaren and Rory with the unbridled backing and encouragement of the marvellous Holywood Golf Club, who made him their youngest-ever member at just eight years old.

Like Lewis when he became World Champion, Rory's modesty, unassuming nature and glowing star quality make him a pin-up for mums, daughters, dads and sons, as well as golfing enthusiasts. Like Lewis, he is an icon who is bringing his sport to new audiences.

Maybe one day we will say that Rory McIlroy is the boy who went some way towards not only saving golf, but breathing new life into what had become a tired, world-weary brand after the fall of the Tiger. Whatever, we are now witnessing the inexorable rise of a brilliant new sporting superstar. So, let's sit back and enjoy it – here's to the next 20 years, Rory!

Frank Worrall

For more information on Frank's bestselling books with John Blake Publishing, please go to www.frankworrall.com

CHAPTER 1

SIMPLY
THE BEST

He would not fail this time. No way. He would not choke; he would not blow it.

Rory McIlroy scratched his forehead underneath his favourite golfing cap, surveyed the green at Congressional, contemplated the day in front of him, smiled at the expectant crowd of fans and press corps from around the world, then teed up for the round that would change his life. Forever.

It was his day of destiny: the final round of the US Open in Bethesda, Maryland. A day and a round that would propel him to world superstardom and prove that he had the makings of the greatest golfer of all time. A day and a round that would leave even the legendary Tiger Woods purring about his talents and potential – and conceding well, yes, the boy from Ulster was a better player than he had been at that age.

A day and a round that would see the Northern Irish wonder-boy golfer Rory McIlroy finally come of age – at the tender age of just 22.

But no, it hadn't all come together out of pure chance, out of random luck. After his meltdown in The Masters at Augusta two months earlier, Rory had taken vital, valuable time out to reassess his game. He had attempted to work out exactly why he had blown up when winning seemed the easier option. Many analysts would voice their fears that the then 21-year-old would never recover from the setback – that he would be forever traumatised by the experience and would find it hard to overcome what they termed 'the inevitable emotional and mental' hurdles. That he would never now go on to win a Major.

Of course, they didn't know the boy; they had confused him with other golfers who had 'bottled it' and afterwards never gone on to triumph in one of the sport's four marquee events. Some mentioned Colin Montgomerie as an example, claiming Rory would go the way of the brilliantly talented, if emotionally brittle Scotsman. To his credit, Monty himself swiftly dismissed the comparison. The Scot, who by then had won 31 tournaments on the European Tour since turning professional in 1987, said he believed Rory would actually learn from the nightmare in Georgia to emerge a stronger, better golfer.

Monty, who never finished higher than second in a Major, observed: 'He's a very young lad and I think he can only learn from this experience. The way he hits the golf ball is second to none. He was playing the best tee to green. Unfortunately the putter let him down from the first hole onwards and it is amazing how small the holes get at Augusta on a Sunday.

'He was probably just trying too hard, trying to achieve what is almost unachievable at that age. He will be back. He has to look at it as a very positive step. With nine holes to go, he was still one ahead at The Masters and that is a very positive thought to take.'

Indeed it was – and the canny Scot also made the very good point that on the day Rory had come up against an opponent at his absolute peak in Charl Schwartzel, as testified by his four birdies on those final four holes at Augusta. Monty astutely observed that putting was of the essence in The Masters and said of the South African: 'I've played with him many times as a European Tour player and was always very impressed with him. He was the best putter of the week and we know at The Masters it is mainly all to do with that.

'His was a name that many Americans had not known and many outside of South Africa and Europe had not heard of. They have now, and that will give him confidence to go forward.'

Despite this, the doom merchants were out in force. In the press, the *Mail*'s brilliant golf writer Derek Lawrenson expressed the fear that many shared when, after Rory's collapse at Augusta, he wrote: 'In the entire history of major championship golf we've rarely witnessed anything like this.

We've seen any number of players choke, we've witnessed plenty more simply not having the skills to cope with the suffocating demands of a Sunday afternoon, but has a man in a position to win ever suffered three holes to match those that befell poor Rory McIlroy in the final round of The Masters on Sunday? Amen Corner they call it, and everyone had better say a prayer for the young Northern Irishman after this disintegration.'

In the *Daily Telegraph*, Oliver Brown continued the theme of Rory needing divine intervention for future success. He opined: 'When Rory McIlroy pitched his ball into Rae's Creek at the 13th he looked fleetingly on the point of tears. No words of consolation, no platitudes that he would be stronger for the sapping and brutal pressure of Masters Sunday could have filtered through to the 21-year-old last night. McIlroy's hideous unravelling, shedding seven strokes in 12 holes when he must have been mentally measuring himself up for the Green Jacket, was not merely Greg Norman-esque. It was the most spectacular – and surely the most affecting – Augusta implosion anyone could remember. As McIlroy crashed and burned at the turn, the patrons thronged around "Amen Corner" were tempted to whisper a prayer for him.'

But Richard Williams of the *Guardian* saw the light through the darkness at Augusta – suggesting Rory might benefit from the collapse to return stronger because he had youth on his side: 'McIlroy did not fade out of the contest. He crashed out of it, brakes gone and tyres screeching, in a welter of debris. Only his youth will help insulate him from

4

the direst consequences of such a terrible, terrifying failure; an older man might never recover. And at least it was relatively quick. Greg Norman's tortured collapse against Nick Faldo in 1996 lasted most of the day.'

CNN's Ben Wyatt also had positive input for Rory, suggesting he might learn from the efforts of Phil Mickelson, if he needed some inspiration: 'There is inspiration close at hand if Rory needs a pick-me-up. Phil Mickelson had been dubbed "the greatest player never to win a Major", having finished second or third between 1999 and 2003. He seemed destined to be an eternal bridesmaid. But "Lefty" clung to a tiny, private thought; a ray of light within him that said he could one day win. And in 2004 he did, at the Augusta Masters; a victory which proved the first of three Masters' triumphs over the next six years. McIlroy can bounce back if he follows the lead set by Mr Mickelson.'

Two months later, at Congressional, Rory would prove the likes of Wyatt, Williams and Montgomerie correct – and quieten the doubters – in securing that wonderful first Major at the US Open. And he would admit that, yes, he had learned from The Masters and the lesson, though painful, was part of the reason why he had triumphed in Bethesda. After his dramatic win, he said: 'Every cloud has a silver lining. What happened at Augusta was a great thing for me in terms of support. It's just been incredible the way people cheered for me the whole week – it feels like a home match. To have that when you come over here and feel like you're one of their own is going to be important in the next few years.

'I felt like I got over The Masters pretty quickly – I kept

telling you guys that, and I don't know if you believed me or not. Nice to prove some people wrong! To be able to finish it off the way I did just tells me that I learned from it and I've moved on. I can always call myself a major champion but now I've got this, I can concentrate on getting some more.'

So, how exactly did he turn it around – from the anguish of Augusta to the unbridled delight of Bethesda – in just two short months to become the youngest European to win a Major in 139 years?

Well, there were two key elements to his remarkable transformation. The first is that the boy is a natural winner. He does not allow himself to become low or depressed if things go wrong; he simply analyses the situation, puts it right and then propels himself forward with a magnificent self-belief that oozes from every pore of his body. This is no moper or sulker, he moves on; the past is history and all that matters is the present and the future, win or lose.

Rory is much of the opinion that you are only as good (or bad) as your last game of golf, so what's the point in getting hung up on days of self-doubt and self-analysis? Sure, a responsible attempt to see why things didn't work out and to look at how to put them right is part and parcel of any top sportsman's make-up but if you allow losses to demoralise and haunt you then you risk their spectre impinging on your next outing on the green – as Colin Montgomerie himself might well point out to be the case.

For Rory, the aim was to get it right next time. As he himself put it, it would be 'nice to prove some people wrong' and to make his critics eat their words. Even in the immediate aftermath of that crushing setback in Augusta, he admitted he would not, nay *could* not, afford to dwell too much on his collapse when he spoke to the press corps on the final day: 'It will be pretty tough for me for the next few days, but I will get over it – I will be fine. There are a lot worse things that can happen in your life. Shooting a bad score in the last round of a golf tournament is nothing in comparison to what other people go through.

'It is a very disappointing day, obviously, but hopefully I'll learn from it and come back a little stronger. It was my first experience of being in the lead going into the last day of a Major, and I felt as if I did OK on the front nine. I was still one shot ahead going into the 10th and then things went all pear-shaped after that, but I'll have more chances, I know that.'

He was also boosted by the knowledge that his growing army of fans worldwide were willing him on to win that first Major after Augusta. After Augusta, the golfing Internet boards were awash with 'hard luck, Rory' messages and 'Come on, you can do it!' before and during the US Open.

As far away as Australia, his supporters were sympathising while The Masters setback sunk in. Down Under, one fan, Andrew Herbert, said: 'I woke up this morning hoping to see him putting on the Green Jacket. Looking, not 1st, 2nd, 3rd. I honestly thought, where is he? Heart sank when I heard about the 80. Pint of Guinness, a ruffling of the hair… Get out there again, mate! A lot of people want you to win, for all the right reasons! Go, Rory!'

And another online well-wisher, PJB, had these words of wisdom for the Northern Irishman: 'While we may be defined by our successes, we are forged in our failures. The Masters is certainly a white-hot crucible and young Mr McIlroy is a ductile piece of metal. He can become the tempered steel that makes the finest blade, he has only to establish his goal and set his mind to it. We saw the elements of a future Masters champion, it is up to him to accomplish according to his aspirations. I wish him well in his experiences.'

And after Bethesda the fans were left in no doubt that a new star had been born. The idea that Rory was actually a golfing saviour was now taking shape: that here, after the dismal spectacle of Tiger Woods' very public demise, was a young man who could take the game forward and indeed open it up to a whole new fan base and encourage people to take it up worldwide.

Golf writer Ray Sanchez suggested as much when he said, 'Do we finally have a new golf superstar in Rory McIlroy? Heaven knows, the sport needs one. Heck, every sport needs one – someone we can root for, look up to, try to follow his or her example. Ever since Tiger Woods went into a tailspin, we've had a long list of faceless champions on the PGA Tour. Rory McIlroy, who's from Northern Ireland, is only 22 years old and it's too early to tell if he's our latest golfer in shining armour. He won the 2011 US Open with a record 16-under-par score last weekend. But one Major does not a superstar make.

'Still, he's young, he's fresh, he can hit the ball a mile – and oh, how he can putt. It was sheer pleasure watching him on television make great shot after great shot. And he's nice looking, friendly, accessible and polite. We can hope.'

One British fan, Andrew Hirst, suggested Rory's success would indeed bring an inevitable and welcome bonus to the membership of golf clubs in the UK: 'From the very first tee he was free-swinging and unlike the tight fairways and water hazards of Augusta, there was nothing in the way of a successful week. But no one could predict the unshakable form he was in. Dropping three shots in four days on one of America's toughest courses proved his class at this level. The new era has begun and it's exciting stuff. After the carnage of Tiger Woods' career left the game in the doldrums we can now move on with a new prince. In recent years, golf memberships have been dwindling and the game lost its credibility for upstanding behaviour and sportsmanship. When the dust settles from this astounding victory it will be the local pro beaming a boyish grin, ready to take the money of a fresh breed of golfer, seeking to emulate their new hero.'

Another also pointed out that the win would boost enthusiasm for golf as a sport, as well as interest in The Open at Kent in July: 'I can't wait for The Open Championship. There's no underestimating the significance of this victory for Rory and the way in which he totally dominated the field. I just hope that The Open is a true reflection of the type of golf that we see in Open Championships. We need a bit of wind to blow across the links and then the real meaning of shot shaping and different types of shots will come to the fore. It would be really symbolic if Rory was to win The Open in testing conditions because no doubt that would reflect the conditions he would have been brought up on in his part of the world. I love watching the best players in the world having to "think" their way around an Open Championship, playing shots that American courses just don't cater for. Punched long irons, little bump and runs, hitting under the wind – it's what golf is all about.'

But for now, that would have to wait. First, Rory wanted to savour the win at Bethesda and was happy to watch re-runs of his triumph and talk to the press about how this had been achieved. He admitted the main thing he had put right after Augusta was his putting. It hadn't required any genius to work that one out – Rory simply shuddered as he recalled his putting nightmare that cost him so dearly in the final round. In particular, he conceded that four-putt double bogey on the 12th would give him a few nightmares for some time to come!

Typical of his straight thinking and positive attitude, he hadn't gone into days of intense analysis and angst over it, though. No, instead he and his father Gerry simply decided to seek out the opinion of a man they trusted implicitly. They asked Dave Stockton, considered one of the best putters of all-time, to help out. The American considered it a privilege and spent a couple of sessions with Rory at the PGA Tour event in Charlotte, North Carolina, at the start of May.

It took Stockton, a former double Major winner and victorious US Ryder Cup captain, next to no time to pinpoint the flaws that were holding back the golfing prodigy. The Californian would later reveal: 'Basically I met with Rory, watched him putting and it took about 10 minutes to fix. I told him, "You're a great ball player and your putting is great." We just needed to work on the mental side of things; it was just a case of getting him into a rhythm. Rory plays through instinct and feel, and that's what's great about him.

'He just needed to line up the ball, look at the hole and the positioning of his feet, and follow through on the putt and keep the back of his left hand going towards the target. His mechanics were flawless but he had to stop concentrating on technique and play what was in front of him.'

By the end of May, the pair met again at the BMW PGA Championship at Wentworth, where Stockton witnessed first hand the improvement in Rory's putting skills. 'When I went to see him at Wentworth, he had already improved and we just brushed up on his putting and chipping,' he said. 'He's a great kid. He's easy to teach, he really is. When I met him he was just 21 years old and he was more like a 35-year-old. If you show him something and he buys into it, he can just do it straightaway.'

There was another element to Stockton's mentoring, too – he knew Congressional well. Indeed, 35 years earlier he had won the 1976 PGA Tournament there. It meant he could pass on tips on how to cope at the course before the event began.

The legendary Jack Nicklaus, too, had a few words of advice for the youngster, telling him to 'put pressure on himself to win.'

Rory would reveal that he had also been inspired by a pre-Congressional trip to Haiti: the young man had gone there in his official capacity as UNICEF's Ireland Ambassador. This journey to the ravaged Caribbean island was his first overseas visit and he was to admit that it had opened his eyes and made him realise that sport was not the be-all and end-all of life. Haiti was still suffering the effects of the earthquake that hit close to the capital, Port-au-Prince, in January 2010.

The Pan American Health Organization (PAHO) estimated between 50,000 and 100,000 people had been killed but as Rory arrived, General Ken Keen – the head military officer in charge of relief efforts in Haiti – commented the total might have been closer to 200,000. And the Red Cross calculated that 3 million – roughly one-third of the country's population – had been directly affected by the quake, with many left homeless.

Rory quickly took in the scale of the devastation, both in human terms with the suffering of those he met and the loss of Haiti's major landmarks – most had been destroyed or significantly damaged. He was told they included the Presidential Palace, the National Assembly and the Port-au-Prince Cathedral (a 1914 structure that took 30 years to build). Other important buildings affected include the country's main jail and a major hospital.

During his two-day trip he was struck by the spirit and determination of the people to rebuild and start again; he was shown newly built schools and camps for those who had lost their homes in the earthquake. He then handed out bars of soap to children at a UNICEF kindergarten and showed them how to wash their hands properly so that they would not become sufferers of cholera, which had already claimed thousands of young lives.

He also visited a UNICEF-funded area, where children could play sports and games. Later, he said: 'It was important to me that my first visit as a UNICEF Goodwill Ambassador be a place like Haiti, where I can see what is being accomplished and what challenges remain.' On the social networking site Twitter, he would reveal how he had been affected by the visit. He first tweeted: 'Pretty emotional day today. Great to see all the work UNICEF do to help and educate kids in this grief-stricken country.' Later, he added: 'My trip to Haiti is coming to an end. Was incredible to see the work UNICEF do here and more importantly, the great spirit the Haitian people have. With the new president and the positivity of the people, a little help could go a long way in this country!'

'Rory was truly moved by what he witnessed in Haiti,' said a source close to the McIlroy camp. 'He met one particular young girl who had lost her father in the quake and whose mother had been seriously injured. He even put up a pic of her on his Twitter site – he found her inspiring because she was so full of life, even though she had lost so much. It helped him at Congressional. He thought of that little girl and the other kids, and their spirit and determination lifted him during the tournament.'

On leaving Haiti, Rory had travelled straight to America to prepare for the US Open, which was scheduled to begin the following week. All the efforts with putting mentor Dave

Stockton and the inspiration garnered from meeting the kids on his trip to Haiti now paid off over the weekend of 16–19 June at Bethesda as he stormed home, setting that new US Open record score of 16-under-par.

He got off to a flier in the first round to immediately seize the tournament by the scruff of its neck when he hit a brilliant first-round six-under-par 65 to take an early three-shot lead. But even after producing six birdies, the perfectionist in Rory was not totally happy with his showing. He remarked: 'To be honest, it could have been better but in the end, I'll take a 65. As for a fast start again, my preparation is a big thing. I always go a week early to the course and play it before many of the others.'

He was referring, of course, to the fact that, at the tender age of 22, he had now taken the lead in all four Majors.

Twenty-four hours later he had completed the first two rounds in a blistering 131 strokes, adding a second-day 66 to his overnight 65. That in itself put him in the record books – he had chalked up the lowest 36-hole total since the US Open's inception in 1895. He also became the first man to go as low as 13-under-par, although he finished the round on 11-under after suffering a double bogey at the last hole.

Clearly, he was aiming to hit the competition at a rasping pace and to put behind him the misery of The Masters. He said: 'The Masters is now history. I'm focusing on this event and trying to win my first Major title; I got over The Masters within a week or so. It all feels quite simple – I'm hitting fairways, hitting greens and holing my fair share of putts – but I'm not letting myself get carried away. We're only halfway through the tournament.' But he was confident there would be no repeat of the blow-up and used his favourite football team, Man United, as an example of how he now fully expected to go on and win. He added: 'Someone told me I'm the same price to win here as Manchester United are to beat West Brom in their first game next season. I'd say United should win – and I've a great chance, too.'

As the second day concluded, former US PGA champ Y.E. Yang appeared the man most likely to close the gap but even he was six shots behind, at five-under-par.

By Saturday, Rory was again ripping up the record books. His third-round 68 meant he had achieved the lowest 54-round total *ever* in the US Open: 199. That was one less than Jim Furyk at Olympia Fields in 2003. Plus his 14-under-par at Congressional was two less than the previous par record in the US Open achieved by Gil Morgan at Pebble Beach in 1992 and Tiger Woods at the same venue in 2000.

Rory's third-round 68 meant he would be going into the final round on the Sunday at 14-under-par with an 8-stroke lead. Yang was still leading the rest of the field at 6-under, while Robert Garrigus, Lee Westwood and Jason Day were tied at 5-under.

Rory's lead has been bettered only three times in all Majors. Tiger Woods and Henry Cotton were 10 in front (at the 2000 US Open and 1934 Open respectively) and Woods 9 ahead at the 1997 Masters. Since the very first Open Championship in 1860, no one has ever lost such an advantage after 54 holes of a Major. The biggest collapse was

Greg Norman in the 1996 Masters: he was 6 clear and lost to Nick Faldo by 5.

Rory said: 'The big goal was to try to get to 15-under. I didn't quite achieve it, but I don't mind. I knew I was going to feel a little bit of pressure and nerves, and it definitely wasn't easy.'

But Westwood still had hope – especially after he was reminded that at the 1966 US Open, Billy Casper was 7 adrift of Arnold Palmer with 9 to play and won in a playoff. After the third round, Westwood observed: 'My mission was to get myself somewhere into the tournament. I said, "Maybe if I can get to 10-under at the weekend" but you don't know how Rory is going to do, how he's going to deal with the big lead. He had a big lead in a major and didn't deal with it well before. There's pressure on him with regards to that, so we'll see.

'They don't give trophies away on Fridays and Saturdays. All I can do is control my game and try and shoot as low a score as possible for me. I drove the ball really well – I think I missed one fairway and one green. I put myself in position to be able to attack the flags. If you drive the ball well around this golf course, it's scoreable.'

Lee was clearly putting on the pressure with the mind games but would he be proved right – that the pressure could get to Rory and he might not be able to deal with it, that he would blow it again, like The Masters?

No chance. He knew it, and so did the rest of the field. Probably even Westwood, if truth be told. Going into his day of destiny, Rory was smiling and clearly contented with his golf. He said: 'I'm feeling good, feeling very good, you know. It's funny to me, it feels quite simple – I really don't know what to say. I put myself in a great position but I know more than probably anyone else what can happen so I've got to stay really focused and try and finish this thing off.'

Relative journeyman (in comparison to Rory, at least) Brandt Snedeker, ranked 46th in the world, summed up the feeling around Congressional that Sunday morning when he said: 'Rory's probably got more talent in his pinkie than I have in my whole body! He is unbelievably talented. I love watching him play because it's a very classical, beautiful golf swing. He's only going to get harder to beat. It's fun to kind of watch him grow up.

'Anybody who makes people want to tune in and watch is a great ambassador and Rory McIlroy makes people want to do that. He's got a great head on his shoulders, which is very hard to do with the amount of success he's had at such a young age. You couldn't ask for a better kid to be out there representing the game.'

It was a splendid tribute from a man with a big heart – and it would prove more than appropriate as Rory roared home that wonderful Sunday in Bethesda of June 2011.

The *Observer*'s Lawrence Donegan set the scene for the final act with some illuminating prose: 'Cautiously aggressive, tentatively tenacious, carefully courageous. Whatever the approach, it worked for Rory McIlroy, who will arrive at Congressional Country Club on Sunday with the promised land of a US Open victory in sight. When Saturday dawned, the unfettered brilliance of the Boy Wonder's opening two rounds had been reined in ever so slightly but only the most blinkered golfing aesthetes could be upset about that. Pragmatists know better.

'What ultimately counts in this utilitarian business of major championship golf are the numbers. It is not how but how many? And in answer to that pointed question, McIlroy returned a 3-under-par 68 for a 54-hole total of 199, 14-under-par. That was good enough for an eight-shot lead over his nearest challenger, Y.E. Yang of Korea, and sensational enough for the historians to sharpen their pencils once again for a little re-writing. Lowest three-round score in the history of the US Open; not bad for a boy from Holywood, Northern Ireland.'

And the fans were just as convinced their man would not let them down now. One commented: 'Stunning − highly enjoyable to watch, from start to finish! Classy saves, very straight irons, more smooth putting, and a complete serenity. The engraver can put his name on the pot now, save himself the last-minute rush tomorrow. I've never enjoyed watching somebody play three days of golf as much as this. He's 14-under and still had so many near misses as well. McIlroy's playing a brute of a course like it is a regular club course rather than the toughest US Open course of all.'

Another applauded Rory for his personable touch, saying, 'What I like about McIlroy is that win or lose, you can imagine him going home tomorrow or whenever and playing a few holes with his mates on Wednesday afternoon. Could you imagine Woods doing that? And he's still a lad! How far is he going to hit the ball when he fills out a bit?

Although what I would love to do even more than hit a drive 200 yards is to be able to play wedge shots like he does. An artist.'

An artist, indeed, but an artist who now had a tougher inner resolve: yes, Rory would finish off the job with all the discipline and command of a golfing assassin, giving his rivals no chance of survival.

McIlroy captured his first Major in style, almost making the final round a lap of honour such was his dominance as he chalked up an eight-stroke triumph. He fired a 2-under-par 69 to finish 72 holes on 16-under-par 268 to claim the 111th US Open. Masters runner-up Jason Day of Australia was second on 276, with Yang Yong-Eun, Lee Westwood and Americans Robert Garrigus and Kevin Chappell sharing third on 278.

Inevitably, there were a few knockers out there – those who claimed Rory had it easy because the rainy weather had left the ground 'playing too soft'. Golf writer Gary Smits quickly put paid to that argument, saying, 'There was a lot of rain in the days before the tournament and during the nights during The Open. Because there had been little rain in the months before, the rough wasn't as thick and juicy as most US Open courses. And while Congressional is a very good course with a lot of history, there aren't a lot of holes that lend themselves to big numbers if a player makes a mistake or two – such as the 10th hole at Augusta National, where McIlroy unravelled and lost his Sunday lead in The Masters.

'Because McIlroy broke every important US Open scoring

record except the 18-hole record and US Opens are supposed to be won with a score somewhere around par, McIlroy's achievement is actually being criticised in some circles but I fail to see how the course not playing as difficult as some Open tracks in the past diminishes McIlroy's week. There won't be an asterisk by his name on the trophy.

'His US Open title means the same as Tiger Woods in 2000 at Pebble Beach, Jack Nicklaus in 1962 at Oakmont, or Ben Hogan in 1951 at Oakland Hills. And I'm pretty sure the $1.35 million check cleared the bank. Maybe he was that good, that week.

'There's an old adage that goes, "You play the ball as it lies and the course as you found it." McIlroy found a course ripe for the taking, and took it. Majors shouldn't have style points.'

Swift praise for Rory's achievement came from the watching Tiger Woods. 'Heck of a performance,' he noted. 'Congrats and well done. Enjoy it. This was an impressive performance.' Injured and licking his wounds after the series of sex scandals that had rocked both his personal life and career, Woods no doubt harked back to 1997 when, as a 21-year-old, he had demolished the field at Augusta to clinch The Masters, the first of his 14 Major triumphs. No doubt he felt the crown slipping, too as Rory made his first claim on it.

Jack Nicklaus also chipped in with a few words of congratulation. 'I think this kid is going to have a great career, no question about that,' the 18-times Major winner said. 'He plays very well. He had a couple disappointments. I didn't think that [Rory's Masters collapse] was going to happen again and it hasn't.'

After his victory, Rory ran to his father Gerry and the two hugged – the culmination of two decades' work finally complete. He then paid tribute to Gerry and all the efforts he had put in – the tripling-up on jobs to help him fund his career, the long journeys to different courses and the constant encouragement – by dedicating the victory to him on Father's Day. Rory said: 'Happy Father's Day, Dad – this one's for you,' after proudly showing off his winning trophy on the course in Maryland.

He then added: 'But I have to mention my mum as well, who's back home watching. I can't thank them enough. As Graeme [McDowell] said last year there will be a few pints of the black stuff going down tonight. I know my friends will be out partying and I can't wait to get back and join them. But the whole week has been incredible. I knew what I needed to do today to win – I put a few new things into practice and it paid off.'

Gerry would later reveal he was 'over the moon' for his son and say that every sacrifice he and wife Rosie had made was now more than worthwhile. He commented: 'We worked very hard to get him where he is. If we had not put the effort in at the time, I could be sitting here wondering what would have happened and regretting not doing it. It was expensive – hotels, airfares and everything – but we worked to get where we are. We are very lucky with Rory.

'Of course there are times everyone gets fed up working,

but as the years went by Rory got better and better, so it was more of an incentive. I didn't mind, and Rosie didn't mind – Rory is our only child so you can just do the best you can for them. We didn't know what was going to happen; all we did was try our best for him. He drove it all, we just helped him – you can't push kids into anything. But once he decided he wanted to do it, we were 100 per cent behind him.'

Gerry also revealed that his now world-famous son was not motivated by money. He added: 'Rory has no interest in money – Rory is just Rory. People find it hard to understand but he doesn't care about cash as long as he has enough to do him. Even growing up he never really cared about money, it has never meant anything to him. He has a nice house nearby and he's put a few quid into it, but apart from that he doesn't spend much.'

That may have been the case but one lucky punter was certainly interested in money – to the tune of almost £20,000 as a result of Rory's triumph. Six years previously the Londoner had bet £300 with William Hill on McIlroy to land a Major before 2020 – at odds of 66:1.

Rory himself was also laughing all the way to the bank – despite an apparent lack of concern about his burgeoning fortune. His win at Congressional earned him a cheque for a cool $1.44 million (£900,000), but in becoming the youngest player to win a Major since Tiger Woods lifted The Masters trophy in 1997, he also set himself up for major riches off the green with sponsorship deals. He already pocketed an estimated $10 million in endorsement deals with Dubai hotels group Jumeirah, Titleist (who supplied his golf balls and equipment) and sunglasses maker Oakley.

Experts predicted he could double that figure when the contracts came up for renewal – and then there were new deals that would inevitably be placed on the table for his inspection. Tiger Woods had earned $92 million in sponsorship in 2009 before his bubble burst and so the 'sky's the limit for Rory' according to the experts. One PR exec, Adrian Rogers, said: 'Rory can step into the gap that has been created by Tiger's demise. He has everything the sport is looking for. He is clean, young, attractive and he connects with the public – which is something Tiger really rarely did, even at the peak of his powers. Tiger is the past; Rory is the future.'

Rory now freely admitted he would 'love to dominate the sport' as his boyhood hero Tiger Woods once had. He had always said that he wanted to emulate Tiger's masterclass of 2000 when he won the US Open by a record 15 shots at Pebble Beach. Now Rory said: 'I know how good Tiger was in 2000 to win by 15 in Pebble. I was trying to go out there and emulate him. I grew up watching him dominate at The Masters in '97, watching him dominate at Pebble in 2000 and St Andrews, and I was just trying to go out there with the same intensity.

'To get one out of the way early, you can always call yourself a Major champion. And hopefully, in the not-so distant future I'll be able to call myself a multiple Major champion.'

Rory had sent records tumbling as he marched home in

glory, becoming the youngest US Open champion since Bobby Jones in 1923 and the youngest Major winner since Woods in 1997.

Tiger had missed out on Congressional with knee and Achilles injuries and now the spin-doctors were busy predicting that Rory was set to replace him, on and off the course, as the new face of the sport with a rash of commercial deals. Rory observed: 'When you win a Major quite early in your career, everyone is going to draw comparisons, it's natural. I don't know if Tiger was watching it on TV, maybe he saw a couple of shots here and there. But it would just be nice for him to be healthy again and get back out on the golf course because he brings something extra to tournaments.

'I've watched Tiger over the last 15 years. When I was growing up, I always had putts to beat Tiger in The Masters or US Open so it would be great to be able to go down the stretch with him one day.'

Certainly that doyen of sports writers James Lawton, commenting in the *Independent*, was in no doubt that Rory was ready to assume Tiger's mantle as the No. 1. In a persuasive piece, he said: '…in a little more than two months he [Rory] had done more than repair the potentially shattering psychological damage of his unravelling on the last day at Augusta when he lost a four-stroke lead in a nightmare of a round of 80 which took him into the shadows of the Butler Cabin, where his earlier brilliance was supposed to have been dressed in the Green Jacket of the US Masters – the fabled reward for the youngest and most demonstrably gifted champion since Tiger Woods claimed the honour 14 years earlier.'

And the *Daily Mail*'s Martin Samuel elegantly set the scene for the new order within world golf when he observed: 'When it was all over, he still used the pontoon bridge to cross the water to the scorer's hut and sign his card; but if Rory McIlroy had chosen to take a short cut, skipping across the shimmering surface, the smart black soles of his still-pristine white shoes barely wet from the encounter, nobody would have been surprised.

'There are some days in the sporting arena that set a young man apart; for McIlroy there are four of them. By most projections, June 16 to June 19, 2011 will be remembered as the time during which golf changed; a movement as significant and irreversible as the passing of the hands of the clock from 11.59pm to midnight each December 31. We are on McIlroy time now. Everything is different from here; or at least it should be.'

One writer even suggested humanity in general could learn from Rory how to deal with personal anguish after his Masters' collapse. Associated Press writer Paul Newberry commented: 'To say J.R. Hildebrand and Rory McIlroy are two of the biggest losers is totally missing the point. Sure, they had unfathomable meltdowns on two of the world's biggest sporting stages – McIlroy at Augusta National, Hildebrand at the Indianapolis 500. But they've come off looking like winners, teaching us all a valuable lesson in how to cope with the realities of a sporting life. Heck, life in general. Someone has to win. Everyone else gets to lose –

sometimes in the most excruciating way imaginable. That doesn't mean you have to look at yourself as a loser. Funny how it took a couple of kids to show us that.'

Rory's fellow golf pros were also convinced here was a young man who could shape the future of the sport and rack up records galore. Prior to the US Open, Ernie Els had said that Rory was 'good enough to change golf history' and there was no shortage of peers willing to step forward and add to this accolade after his mighty win at Bethesda.

Three-times Major winner Padraig Harrington predicted Rory might even top the 18 Majors won by his mentor Jack Nicklaus. Harrington had known for years that Rory would be some player – and even when he won the 2007 Open at Carnoustie gave a nod to the youngster he believed would one day be the best around. As he collected the Claret Jug, he laughed, looked over at Rory (who had won the silver medal as the highest finishing amateur) and quipped: 'I'm just glad to have won this before Rory gets going!'

After the 2011 US Open, Harrington was equally effusive, saying: 'Rory is 22 years old and if you are going to talk about someone challenging Jack's record, there's your man. Winning Majors at 22 with his talent, he'd have at least 20 more years so probably another 100 more Majors in him where he could be competitive. That would give him a great chance.

'Rory has proved in playing the Majors so far that he is comfortable making the scores and he's managed to lead after 18 holes, 36 holes and 54 holes and 63 holes, so now all he has to do is get another nine holes.'

And fellow Ulsterman Graeme McDowell, his close friend who had triumphed at the US Open a year earlier, also got in on the act. Graeme handed him the trophy and observed: 'It's just phenomenal – you run out of superlatives to describe what he has done this week. He's decimated a field. I've been waiting for this to happen. He's that good, there's no doubt about it. I first heard about him when he shot 61 at my home course in Portrush. You hear rumours about people and good players, but this kid is something special.

'His swing is phenomenal – he's got the full package as far as his golf game is concerned, if his putter behaves itself. Tiger's something very special. He had it all – the mental capacity, the short game, the putter. If Rory adds a couple of weapons to his arsenal, he can be as good.'

Finally, the people who mattered most to Rory on the circuit – the fans – chipped in with a variety of tributes to their hero. Probably the most eloquent of all was by someone who called himself 'A Happy Rocket' and who, like many of the pros, made the point that Rory's emergence signalled a changing of the guard at the very top of the sport. The fan said: 'Firstly, the most unbelievable display of golf, power, control, imagination, everything I've ever seen – bar nothing Woods has done, and that's saying something. Second, it's a matter of time before McIlroy gets to No. 1, probably after he wins at St George's next month.

'Third, it's so refreshing to see what's happening in the sport after a decade of players happy to tag along in Woods' slipstream, making a million for finishing 100th on tour (not their fault, it's only human nature). Now a batch of kids who

27

had Woods as their hero are bursting on the scene and gunning for HIM like he gunned for Jack.

'Woods is history – he may well win another Major, but he's history in more ways than one. Nobody cares about him any more, not Rory, Schwartzel, Oosthuizen, Kaymer, Donald, Manassero, Ishikawa or another host of 19–23-year-olds in white belts, pounding it for miles and putting like God.

'Think of your own club – how much better is it when "the best player" is a nice guy, humble when he wins, gracious when he loses, than a brat who nobody likes but has talent to waste. Woods can leave the scene anytime he likes with his language, club throwing and spitting and leave the way [open] for a whole new crop who respect the game and more importantly respect each other while trying their hearts out. Sit back and enjoy the next five years – it's been a long time coming.'

The blueprint for the future had been cast but first, let's turn back the clock and travel back in time to learn about the childhood roots, the upbringing, the family values and the golfing journey formed from early steps as a toddler armed with a plastic club that was to mould young Rory McIlroy into the man who would become a champion and a potential golfing saviour.

CHAPTER 2

THE GENTLE HAND FOREMOST

Rosie McIlroy would come to dread the mornings when their son woke up early, screaming for attention in his bedroom. She had told Gerry it was a fanciful notion to expect Rory to become a golfing prodigy just because he was crazy about the sport. And she had ticked her husband off – though always with a tut-tut and a smile – when he bought the boy a plastic golf club. She was not smiling now, though, as he stood up wailing at the side of his bed, determined to grab her or Gerry's attention – and swinging the club from side to side as she approached to soothe him. A couple of times, the toddler would accidentally catch her with it as she tried to grab him and comfort him – and she would scold her husband for 'buying him the bloody thing in the first place.'

Not that she really meant it, of course. 'He was holding a

golf club before he could walk,' she would recall years later. 'He'd be sitting in the pram with a plastic golf club in his hand. That's the way we were woken up — banged over the head with a plastic golf club!' Rosie McIlroy knew her son was special; that he had golfing genius in his blood from the day he was born and that her husband was correct in encouraging him towards the sport from infancy. Even if it meant that at the age of two he would have a hissy fit with his plastic golf club after waking up in the middle of the night. Yes, Rory McIlroy was born to be the King of Golf.

Gerry McIlroy (then 27) had married Rosaleen McDonald (27) in St Colmcille's Church in Holywood, East Belfast, County Down on 13 January 1988. A year and a half later, on 4 May 1989, their son Rory was born — also in Holywood — and would be baptised in the church where they were wed. He was to be their only child and from the age of 10 months began to show glimpses of the God-given talent bestowed on him; they in turn would become proud of him and devote themselves through the years to helping him make his dream of being a professional golfer come true. Later, in Rory's formative years as a golfer, Gerry would work up to 100 hours a week — cleaning toilets and showers at a local rugby club in the mornings and bartending at the golf club in the afternoon and evenings — and Rosie would clock on for the night shift at a local factory packaging millions of rolls of tape.

Back in his days as a toddler, they sent Rory to St Patrick's, a Catholic primary school where, to this day, his first Communion photograph still hangs on a wall. Rory was a happy child and would later admit he had a contented upbringing, mostly oblivious to the Sectarian Troubles that had for decades haunted the nation. His parents were determined that he would not become scarred and that he would grow up to be a young man who was a credit to his nation, who would cross the Protestant/Catholic divide and bigotry. They did a good job, too: his family may have been Catholic and Rory would grow up with their teachings – of peace and people working as one rather than bitterly divided – but would refuse to be defined by his faith. He would one day admit that one of his major wishes was to be viewed as someone who had overcome all the traditional wranglings of Catholic and Protestant, Irish and British.

Of course, just five miles away in the centre of Belfast the scene was far different – with daily riots and bombs going off – from the relative peace of Holywood where Rory was growing up, but the McIlroy family would still have their own personal reminder of the Troubles that raged in their homeland. Seventeen years before Rory was born, in 1972, his great-uncle Joe was murdered by a UVF hit squad for moving into a protestant area of East Belfast. He lies in the same church in which Rory was baptised and where Gerry and Rosie were married.

To a large extent Rory was shielded from the Troubles by the very fact that he was lucky enough to grow up in Holywood. It was a small, quintessentially middle-class coastal town with just over 12,000 inhabitants and Gerry was determined his boy would have chances in life that he and his family had not been granted. The political commentator Newton Emerson best summed up how Rory lived near the Troubles but had managed not to be personally affected by them when he wrote in the *Irish Times*: 'It is just five miles from Rory McIlroy's house in Holywood to the riot-torn streets of East Belfast, yet it might as well be a world away. Nowhere else in the world has a young champion golfer ever lived this close to a riot, except when Tiger Woods lived in Hollywood during the 1993 LA riots. So, strictly speaking a young champion golfer has never lived in a town called Holywood with one "L" just five miles from a riot. But still, picture the contrast between the young man playing golf and the young men throwing golf balls. Powerful stuff.'

Gerry had a hunch that his boy's big break in life might well be in golf – the game he and his family had adored for many years. The sport was something they did know about, something they could pass on with pride.

That devotion to the game began with Rory's grandfather Jimmy, who repaired cranes in the Belfast docks where *RMS Titanic* was built. His real love was golf and he proved his talent at weekends when he played at the Holywood club that has now become synonymous with young Rory's success. Jimmy was one of the club's top players and his enthusiasm and love for golf encouraged his sons – Rory's father, Gerry, and his uncles, Colm and Brian – to also take up the sport. Gerry, like Jimmy, would prove the man to beat – a natural, but also a player who dedicated hours to improving his game.

In the years to come, those long hours on the course and

the driving range would prove well spent for Gerry would now become the driving force behind his only son's ambitious bid to become the best golfer in the world, let alone Holywood. It was a mission that would not have been possible but for the efforts of Gerry and Rosie, as Rory himself would admit after he won the US Open in 2011.

The mission began as soon as Rory could crawl and would end with that remarkable win at Congressional, nearly 22 years later. When Rory was born, Gerry was already working as a barman at the Holywood Golf Club – a job that came with the perk of allowing him to indulge his own love of the game. Some days he would bring young Rory with him and when he had finished his shift and ventured out onto the greens, the youngster would look on from his pram as his dad hit balls around the course. 'It was quite amazing,' a source recalled, 'the little lad would sit there looking on, as if hypnotised by what he was seeing. Club members would often comment about it – that they hadn't seen a little 'un so engrossed in the game. It was as if he was a natural and was just waiting to grow a bit older so he could finally have his go, too.'

And that wouldn't be far off. Before he was a year old, Rory was crawling around the green, following his dad's progress and within another year, driving everyone mad with his own set of plastic clubs and balls – including Rosie, when he woke up during the night!

By the age of 18 months, Gerry was already busy teaching his son about the game and the toddler would often practise at his great-aunt Frances McDonald's home in Scarva Road,

Banbridge. Indeed, Frances took one of the first action shots of the boy who was to become a golfing superstar on her own back lawn. 'He first played with his wee putter on my back lawn,' she would later recall. 'I remember him well in that wee Aran jumper – he could barely hold the club.' Her son Paul, a keen golfer himself, also has fond memories of those days.

'I remember him coming down to the house like it was yesterday,' he would tell the *Banbridge Leader*. 'He loved golf from an early age and I remember him with his wee plastic clubs.'

By the age of two, Rory was hitting 40-yard drives and although he also liked to play football with his mates on the street corner outside the family home in Holywood, golf was to remain his first love. Soon, golf became the No. 1 factor in his life as he started to spend more time at Holywood Golf Club (which he still retains as his home course to this day and credits with providing an ideal base to become a top player). He was proposed for club membership and at the tender age of eight, became Holywood's youngest-ever member. 'Everyone at the club knew him by then,' says a source close to Holywood. 'And everyone knew he was a prodigy – and a potential genius in the making. We knew we were witnessing something very special with this young boy, it was an exciting time.'

Rory started his early training with Michael Bannon, the former head golf pro at the club. 'I suppose when he was about 5 or 6 you sort of knew there was something special there,' Bannon later observed. 'And he was so good when he was 7½ years of age that one of the men in the golf club came out and asked me, what do you think of Rory? Can he join the golf club? So, Holywood Golf Club let him become a member at 8 years of age.'

Robert Cooley, 62, a member of the club for 25 years, would later tell the *Daily Mail*, 'His talent was recognised at such a very young age. You could see there was something special there. He had a self determination from an early age to want to be a golf professional – not only a golf professional, he wanted to be the best golf professional. He could drive the ball forever, chip the ball better, he was a great putter. He has an analytical brain, and he has the mettle and fortitude to be the best.'

Rory was also doing well at primary school and was a popular boy, well liked by his teachers and fellow pupils. The former were amazed when they learnt what a golfing prodigy they had in their midst – especially when he won the Under-10 World Championship at Doral in Florida while finishing the course with five shots less than any of the other 80 youngsters taking part!

Such trips abroad did not come cheap and this is where Gerry and Rosie's devotion to their son that manifested itself with hard work really started to count. Already Rory was making a name for himself but he also proved to be a real student of the game from an early age. He watched endless tournaments on TV with Gerry and studied the techniques of his favourite golfers – players such as Nick Faldo – on videos. Always, he was eager to learn and digest as much information as he could. Instinctively, he knew early on that if he was to be the best, he would have to work hard at his game and take in as many tips on how to improve it as he could.

At nine years old, Rory notched his first hole in one and also starred on a Northern Ireland TV show, hitting golf balls into a washing machine – just as he was now regularly doing at home (much to his mum Rosie's bemusement). A year later, after he put a copy of his hero Tiger Woods' scorecard from the 1997 Masters on his bedroom wall (along with a poster of the No. 1 player of the time), he would also bemuse the pros at Holywood by filling out his own scorecards at Holywood. He signed the cards 'Rory Nick Faldo McIlroy' in a salute to another of his favourite golfing stars. 'The thing about Rory is when he was growing up and you asked him questions, he'd give you these very definite straight answers and it was stuff you couldn't laugh [at],' Bannon would tell ESPN, 'Well, I never did because I always knew someday this guy could do it.'

When the time came to step up to secondary school, Rory moved to Sullivan Upper – a religiously mixed grammar establishment. Gerry and Rosie had been impressed by its values and motto, which is printed on pupils' blazers – *Lámh Foisdineach An Uachtar*. Irish for 'with the gentle hand foremost', it served to support their ambition for Rory to grow up in a new Northern Ireland, one forged through peaceful means in which conflict had no place to thrive.

Rory settled into his new school and continued to prove more adept at golf than lessons. Aged 11, he shot level par at

Holywood Golf Club and then spent the summer of 2000 playing the game in America. He took part in 10 junior tournaments organised by the Utah Junior Golf Association – and didn't win any of them! The previous year, when he won the Under-10 World Champion in Florida, he had met a boy called Scott Pinckney. Scott had told him all about the events in Utah and afterwards Rory pestered his parents to allow him to go over to the States for the summer. Eventually they relented, keen for their son to develop both as a person and a golfer, and so he stayed with Scott's family.

Despite failing to win at the events, Rory had a great summer: he was becoming a stronger person and a more independent spirit, although he would always remain loyal and steadfast to his parents and family. He loved the lifestyle in America and enjoyed his stay with the Pinckneys. Scott's father, Doug, would reveal that there was only one real moment of panic during the entire stay – when one particular day, away from the tournaments, Rory forgot to slap on some sun cream as protection from the constant scorching hot weather. He had gone swimming with Scott and some other friends and ended up with blisters all over his shoulders. 'I had to call his parents about that one,' Doug recalled.

By the age of 13, Rory was a scratch handicap golfer and it was becoming clear to all and sundry connected with his development that he was shaping up as an excellent prospect – a player who would not only have a decent career one day but who might also reach the very top of the golfing trees and even win Majors.

By the age of 15, he and his parents began seriously examining his options. Should he stay on at school beyond 16 and try to achieve academic success? Or would he be better served leaving early to concentrate on a golfing career that was already suggesting massive rewards? He was no academic genius and no dunce either – but he was a golfing genius, no doubt about it. Eventually, he would choose to opt out early in the summer of 2005, just before taking his GCSEs – it was a brave decision and one that would pay huge dividends. However, the choice was quite logical when you consider just how brilliant he was at the game of golf.

Years later, talking about his time at Sullivan, Rory would tell youngsters at his former school: 'A few of the teachers will tell you I probably wasn't the best pupil you've ever seen.' He also admitted that he found it difficult to concentrate on schoolwork, given his dedication to golf: 'It was tough – I was away quite a lot so every time I came back, I was always trying to catch up. It was very tough to try to balance everything but I tried my best. All I wanted to do was play golf and I knew by the time I was 15 or 16 that that was the path I was going to take.'

Jon Stevenson – headmaster at Sullivan Upper during Rory's time there – remarked: 'He was always a prodigious golfer and it was no great surprise when he became a professional golfer, it was always his intention. The talent was always there, people who knew about golf knew he was fantastically talented and it was a case of when he would turn professional and what route he would take.

'It is no surprise that he has reached the dizzy heights he

has, maybe somewhat earlier than people may have expected. I think the talent is a given with Rory. The question mark has been about his attitude and maybe his character but he has two tremendous attributes: this boy really learns, on top of that he has got steely determination.'

And the school's current headmaster Chris Peel revealed that Rory had always been destined for golfing stardom; that he was a boy who was determined to reach the top and happy to put in all the hours needed to become a great, working on technique and approach. Peel revealed that even from day one at Sullivan, Rory made it clear to himself and his fellow teachers that golf was the mainstay of his life. When, aged 11, he had been asked to write about his hopes and dreams, he simply stated: 'I am a keen golfer and I hope to get on the golf team.'

And he would do just that – and much more. A month after leaving school, in the July of 2005, Rory would prove that, yes, he had made the right decision to quit his studies early and lay down a dramatic marker for the future as he smashed the course record at a prestigious course in an amateur tournament. Rory McIlroy was on his way to the top. The former schoolboy was growing up – and fast – and now nothing and no one would hold him back.

CHAPTER 3

AMATEUR
POWER

Rory was just 16 years and two months old when he shocked both pros and media analysts alike with his showing at Royal Portrush (which had hosted the 1951 Open) on the north coast of Northern Ireland. He was taking part in the North of Ireland Amateur Open at the world-famous course in July 2005 when he hit an 11-under-par round of 61. That amazing round included nine birdies and an eagle – and it bettered the previous record by three shots.

Rory was delighted with his round, labelling it 'unbelievable'. 'To shoot 61 anywhere is great – but to shoot it around Royal Portrush is even better,' he told the BBC. 'It was a great experience.'

Dese Hassan of Royal Portrush observed: 'It was a

marvellous performance by anybody but for a 16-year-old boy to go round one of the major links in the world in 61 shots – 33 out and 28 back and 26 putts – is phenomenal.'

It was also the round that pushed him into the limelight: from now on no one would ask who he was, or if he had the potential to be a great. But even before that he had been setting the amateur world alight while still a schoolboy at Sullivan High.

In 2001 and 2002 he won the Ulster Boys' Under-15 championship and was then victorious in the same event's Under-18 championship of 2003 and 2004. In 2004 he was also crowned Ireland's Junior Sports Personality of the Year.

Also, at 15 he had been a member of Europe's winning 2004 Junior Ryder Cup team. The tournament was held in Ohio, USA: the Europeans were defending the trophy and attempting to win it for the fourth time in five years. It took place at the Westfield Group Country Club in Westfield Centre, Ohio, on 11–12 September, the week before the 35th Ryder Cup matches in Michigan. The two teams comprised six boys, aged 16 and under, in a Ryder Cup-style competition that brought together juniors from Europe and the United States in a biennial contest first played in 1995.

The 2004 European side was decided at the European Young Masters, which had taken place in Austria, and Rory would be working under the captaincy of Andy Ingram, former skipper of the Welsh boys team and full international side until 2003. The boys' team comprised Dominic Angkawidjaja of Austria, Luis Garcia del Moral (Spain), England's Oliver Fisher, Zachariah Gould (Wales),

Marius Thorp (Norway) and Rory, of Northern Ireland. They faced a United States team captained by Will Mann, who had served as president of the PGA of America from 1998 to 2000.

There was certain precedence of how important the tournament could be in helping youngsters to the big time and Rory knew if he did well, it would be an enormous boost to his career. He only needed to glance back at the inaugural Junior Ryder Cup matches – which featured a 15-year-old Sergio Garcia – to see this could be the case.

Rory played his part as Europe beat America 8½ to 3½ to lift the trophy. The Europeans, leading 4½ to 1½ after the Saturday fourballs, won the first three matches in the second and final day of match play. Overall, Europe had 65 birdies compared to the USA's 46.

Rory had become the first Irishman to play in the Junior Ryder Cup and afterwards he was buzzing with joy. 'It was a very good experience. All the team played very well,' he observed, after taking half a point from his two fourball matches. The uplifting experience wasn't over yet, though: he and the rest of the juniors headed for Detroit to watch the seniors lift the Ryder Cup with a record 18½–9½ margin at Oakland Hills on the Sunday.

Rory cheered on his compatriot Darren Clarke and when asked what he felt about the double triumph by the juniors and the seniors, purred: 'Brilliant – my aim now is to win Majors and hopefully play in the Ryder Cup.' The boy was hardly short of confidence or ambition.

A year later he became the youngest-ever winner of both

the West of Ireland Amateur Championship and the Irish Close Championship. He won the West of Ireland Amateur Golf Championship at Rosses Point, defeating David Finn 2&1 in the final at the County Sligo Club. In the morning semis, he had already seen off the challenge of Rory Leonard by a hole.

Three months later, he kept up the winning habit by taking the title at the Irish Close Amateur Championship by beating Galway's Eddie McCormack 3 and 2 in the final at Westport. In doing so, he created another bit of history: becoming the first player to hold the Irish Close and West of Ireland amateur titles since Garth McGimpsey won both titles in 1988.

In 2006 he would retain the West of Ireland Championship and followed that up with back-to-back wins at the Irish Close Championship. Rory was 'over the moon' with his 3 and 1 West of Ireland win at County Sligo Golf Club, saying this meant more to him than his first triumph, a year previously: 'It's definitely more special to defend the title. It was an accomplishment to win it last year but there was a lot more expectation on me this time. I'm absolutely shattered!'

He had overcome the challenge of England international David Horsey in the semis – and what a challenge it was. Indeed, Rory was to admit afterwards that it was 'the toughest match' he had ever played. It appeared he might be packing his bags early as Horsey set off at a cracking pace with three birdies in the first five holes but he hung on in there and gradually ground his opponent down with a fine display and by keeping his nerve in a tense playoff.

Rory admitted: 'It was so tight. But the putter behaved well all week. Every time I needed to get a putt, I holed it. For the last two months' solid I've been working on my putting.

'I changed my stroke after Dubai with the help of Niall Manchip and it's made a huge difference. It was vital too, because my long game wasn't as good as it usually is this week. The 17th has been nice to me this week – last year I made a few double bogeys on it. But after the 18th I really calmed down and played well in the playoff; I was really nervous before that.'

In May 2006, Rory was all pumped for the Irish Amateur Open. He desperately wanted to win the event as he was aiming to complete a rare double at Portmarnock. If he won The Open, he would become the first player since Tom Craddock in 1959 to hold both the Irish Amateur Close and Open titles at the same time. But Rory was no fool – he knew winning the 72-hole strokeplay tournament would be a tough nut to crack as he was up against a strong international field. He said: 'I held the Irish Boys, the Irish Close and the Irish Youths titles at the same time last year, so to hold the Close and this one at the same time would be pretty sweet. There's a great field here but it's a very fair golf course and I am playing and driving the ball well, so I think I have a very good chance.'

It was a sign of his growing confidence – and impact – that some players were now starting to speak out against him. One was Welsh Walker Cup veteran Nigel Edwards, who seemed to think Rory needed pulling down a peg or two.

Edwards growled: 'There are many good players in the field, not just him. I would have thought there are probably 20 who can win. All of Ireland are pinning a lot of hopes on him but believe it or not, there is a world outside Rory McIlroy. There is a lot of talk about him and he has done very well, but there are another 119 players who have a chance, too.'

Rory had finished third in the previous week's Lytham Trophy but felt he had a good chance at Portmarnock – despite anything the likes of Edwards might say. He admitted: 'I was disappointed not to win at Lytham but it just gives me more motivation to go out and win this week. Portmarnock is not as tight as Lytham – it is more enjoyable and there is a good variation of long and short holes. I'm looking forward to it.'

But it was not to be: in a nail-biting playoff, Rory would lose out to Finland's Antti Ahokas. The Finn had started the final day two strokes ahead of him, but Rory's third-round 74, joint-lowest score of the morning, had them even and heading for a three hole playoff at the first, second and ninth holes. Both made par on the first hole but Ahokas remained the calmer of the two and would go on to triumph, thus becoming the third successive overseas winner of the Irish Amateur Open. For Rory, the depressing final result read like this: 291 R. McIlroy (Holywood) 73 71 74 73, A. Ahokas (Finland) 71 71 76 73 (Ahokas won after three holes aggregate playoff over first, second, ninth – Ahokas 4 4 3; McIlroy 4 4 4).

A month later, Rory would put the disappointment

behind him as he retained his Golfsure Irish Amateur Close championship, beating Simon Ward 3 and 2 to become the first player since Joe Carr (1965) to win back-to-back Close titles.

He had beaten Connor Doran's 2 and 1 in the semis. The previous year, the duo met at the same stage but this time around Rory was victorious after halving the hole in par 4s at the 17th.

In the final, Rory appeared in trouble when he let slip an early two-hole lead. But he came storming back at the 9th hole, regaining the lead when Ward missed the green on the left, pitched to 8ft and missed the putt for his par.

Rory went 2 ahead with a birdie three at the 10th and retained that lead after the 11th and 12th holes were halved in par fours. The long 13th was also halved, in par fives. At the short 14th, the defending champion increased his lead with a par but Ward came back with a winning par four at the 15th, which reduced his deficit to two holes with three to play. The end came at the 16th, where he triumphed by holing a 40ft birdie putt.

Afterwards, Rory admitted that he sometimes struggled in matches because of lapses in mental application: 'At times I play games with myself because of complacency, not boredom. The key to the week was that I drove it very well – long and straight. And my putting was good as well. That was it, really.'

Bigger and more prestigious titles loomed – especially when he became European amateur champion in August of the same year at Biella Golf Club, near Milan, Italy. Rory beat England's Stephen Lewton by three strokes with a final score of 274 (65-69-72-68). Golf instructor and writer Deepak Acharya, based in Kathmandu, Nepal, recalled the day with fondness and marked the youngster down as a player to watch out for in the future, someone who could go on to achieve great things: 'The first encounter I had with superstar golfer Rory McIlroy was in August 2006 at the European Amateur Championship at Biella Golf Club, near Milan in Italy. I was not even interested in watching his game until he posted a 65 on the first round of the Championship, then I decided to introduce myself and followed his game, too. Later, he went on to win the Championship. He was only 17 years but brought to mind another superstar golfer, Sergio Garcia, who had won the same tournament at the age of 15. I found him an extremely confident ball striker.'

Yes, Rory's reputation was certainly growing – and on a worldwide scale, too. The same year he also scooped a series of prestigious Sports Star of the Year awards from three of Ireland's best newspapers – the *Irish Examiner*, the *Irish Independent* and the *Belfast Telegraph*. 'He had the Midas touch, even in his teens,' says a source. 'He was a winner, pure and simple – he went out on the greens and came back as champion. Everything he touched seemed to turn to gold. The boy was pure dynamite on the courses, nothing and no one could touch him or stop him. It was just a matter of time before he turned pro and started racking up the wins on that circuit.'

It was indeed but for now he would continue to make his mark as an amateur and he would end this stretch of his budding career with the highest accolade available when he topped the world rankings. But first, in October 2006, Rory represented Ireland in the Eisenhower Trophy, the amateur world team championship.

It would be some feat to even finish in the Top 10 – a total of 70 teams, the most ever in the history of the championship, would be taking part in the event in South Africa. These included eight new teams: Bosnia and Herzegovina, Botswana, Bulgaria, Gabon, Honduras, Mauritius, Morocco and Namibia. And it wasn't as if Rory would necessarily be up against fellow youngsters – Roberto Gomez of Brazil was making his record-breaking 12th appearance in the tournament at the age of 49! Ireland finished tied 9th at the end of the tournament and Rory declared he had enjoyed the experience and that it had been another invaluable learning curve in his development.

But there would be disappointment in 2007 when he crashed out of the West of Ireland Championship at Rosses Point, failing in his bid to win the title for three years in a row. A birdie at the last hole by quarter-final rival Paul Cutler ended his dream. Rory would admit: 'I didn't putt the best this week. That was the big difference – and it was the one I really wanted to win, so I'm disappointed.'

On 6 February 2007 he topped the World Amateur Golf Ranking, though he lost the top spot after just one week before regaining it a month later. That No. 1 spot was reclaimed after his brilliant individual performances in the Grey Goose Cup (formerly known as the Sherry Cup) in Spain. He won the Cup and was thrilled as he had now emulated Padraig Harrington and Sergio Garcia in winning the individual title at the European Nations Championship at Sotogrande. McIlroy had opened with a 69 to share second place – in a tie with Maurius Thorp of Norway and Belgium's Xavier Feyaerts on 3-under-par and just one stroke behind Dane Peter Baunsoe.

He was just as pleased that the win put him back at the top of the amateur world rankings but it had been a tense finish as he triumphed over Thorpe in a sudden death situation, ending Ireland's 16-year search for a winner (the last being Harrington in 1991). Rory would not be making it a double cause for celebration: his Irish team lost out by just one stroke for the team title to the Danish, finishing tied 2nd with England. The final top three in the team results read like this: 863 Denmark: P. Drost (75) 76 73 67; P. Baunsoe 68 (80) 68 (77); R. Nielsen 73 71 (75) 74; N. Rasmussen 73 77 73 70. 864 Ireland: R. McIlroy 69 70 70 72; S. Ward 71 73 (76) 73; S. Lowry (76) 72 75 70; N. Kearney 74 (77) 75 (74); 864 England: G. Wolstenholme 71 74 (72) 69; E. Richardson (81) 74 71 72; P. Waring 74 73 71 71; M. Cryer 72 (74) 72 (76).

But Rory had one last big tournament to play before he could say goodbye to his amateur status. It was another Irish team event – this time the Walker Cup. The *Guardian*'s Lawrence Donegan summed up the mood of expectation surrounding the youngster, who had already competed in two pro events (more of those in the next chapter) and was beginning to draw in the crowds with his brilliant golf and warm personality: 'If the outcome of the 2007 Walker Cup is too close to call then there is very little doubt about which player will attract the most attention when the contest between the best amateurs from the US and Great Britain and Ireland tees off at Royal County Down club today.

'Rory McIlroy has already made his mark on the professional game this summer at Carnoustie, where he was tied for third place after the first round and made the cut at The Open, winning the silver medal as the best amateur. But this weekend's contest represents the 18-year-old Irishman's last chance to make an impression on the amateur game. [It] is McIlroy who has caught the imagination, not least because of his free-spirited approach.'

Now 18, Rory had been 'chuffed' to be named in the Great Britain and Ireland team to face the United States in the event – especially as it would be staged at Royal County Down in his home county. Tony Disley, chairman of the R&A selection committee, said McIlroy was in there on merit: 'We have picked a strong team that is more than capable of defeating the Americans. The team not only includes players with experience at the highest level but has a number of exciting younger players, who we believe will excel on the occasion.'

Home captain Colin Dalgleish added: 'Rory has a sound technique and great flair. It's a great and amazing coincidence to have somebody of Rory's exceptional talent to come along when the matches are being played in County Down. We're expecting great things of him but Rory gets no special privileges.'

For Rory, the welcome from the thousands of home fans

who turned out to greet him would never be forgotten. 'He was so grateful and appreciative,' a source confirms. 'He loves the fans who get behind him from Northern Ireland and felt a very special bond with them over the two days, as he always does when they turn out for him. It was a very special weekend for him on home territory – it was just a pity that the result didn't match the occasion.'

Indeed it was. But there was massive expectation and enormous stress, as outlined by a general press/GB&I press question and answer session *before* the tournament. The type of questions and the answers from Rory and team-mate Lloyd Saltman and captain Dalgleish sum up the unique pressures of the occasion. Here is a selection of the Q&As illustrating the situation facing young Rory:

Q. 'Rory, your point of view about the GB&I players, what do you know about the US Team and have you got any views about the American players at all that you're going to be facing this weekend?'

RORY McILROY: 'I lost the US Amateur final last week on TV and Colt [Knost] is a very good player, has a good ball flight, very penetrating ball flight. And they are all very good players. If they weren't, they wouldn't be on the team. I think, you know, I played with Kyle Stanley before at the Orange Grove a couple of years ago, and Rickie Fowler is another good young player. Jamie Lovemark as well; a couple of the guys from the Ireland team, I actually played with them last year at the Western Amateur and they said he's just going to be a fantastic player. I think there's a lot of really good individuals on that team and it's going to be tough for us this week.'

Q. 'And Rory, you know this course better than anybody – what is the secret to playing?'
RORY McILROY: 'I think the good thing about the three times we've been here is we've played the course in different conditions. It's going to be very beneficial for us because I know the forecast looks pretty good but you never know what's going to happen. So I think it was good that we got to play the golf course in different conditions. I think the thing about it is just hit it on the fairway, hit it on the green, don't do anything fancy. It's the sort of course like, if you just play the front half of the greens, you're going to have a chance. You know, there's going to be a lot of holes over par as well. It's just that sort of golf course if you short-side yourself or you miss it. There's a lot of run-offs and fall-offs to the greens, as well.

'Yeah, I mean, I think the thing is, everyone said if you play the front of the green and take your chances from there, likelihood is you make pars on the difficult holes, 50 per cent of the time you're going to win those holes.'

Q. 'The first Walker Cup is obviously a pretty nerve-wracking occasion and you've also got the home crowd factor for you; how much benefit was Carnoustie and how are you approaching the week?'

RORY McILROY: 'People have made comparisons about Carnoustie and this week, but I think it's completely different. You're playing for nine other guys out there. The crowds at Carnoustie were pretty awesome, but I think this week's just going to be so much better for me and for everyone else.

'It's a bit more – the crowds walk with you on the fairway and stuff, and I'm just really looking forward to it and I can't wait to get started.'

Q. 'Rory, Lloyd, how do you feel about playing with so many spectators behind you in the fairway and inside the ropes? It's unusual, so many – how do you think it will affect you?'

LLOYD SALTMAN: 'It's a good thing. We've played amateur golf obviously all year to get onto this team. You know, we're used to sometimes at some of the events, you get a bit of a crowd and stuff, and that is amateur golf. They walk with you and they feel right involved.

'We hear the marshals are going to have pretty good control, so on the greens we'll have space and when we are on the fairway they will be behind us. It's not going to bother us and it's great to have the home support – a lot of people will be out here watching Rory and stuff like that, which will be great. So they will probably all be around him – 9,000 and a bit of a gap, a thousand around us – so we should be fine. It's great. It's quite a good change to play hands-on and most of the majority will be supporting us, so no complaints.'

RORY McILROY: 'To add to that as well, I think when the crowds walk with you on the fairways, it creates a better atmosphere as well. There's really no way to describe it. I actually like the crowds to walk with you on the fairway – it just creates a buzz around the place. I think that one of the things we're all really looking forward to is the amount of people that are going to be here. I think that the atmosphere on the first tee come Saturday morning is going to be electric. I think we are really looking forward to that.'

Q. 'Lloyd and Rory, the last time I looked, the bookies had you as odds-on favourite. Is that something you would agree with, or is that a burden for you or something that you think is justified?'
RORY McILROY: 'No, I mean, it depends – I don't know. I think some people don't really know a lot about the American team and you really can't underestimate them because I mean, they are all fantastic players.

'As I said, it's going to be really tough for us but I think we've got a good chance – I'm sure the Americans are very adaptable and there are a few linksy courses over there, anyways, so I'm sure they know how to play golf courses like this.'
LLOYD SALTMAN: 'I think it's quite a good thing because if people favour us that's why we worked so hard all year to get on the team, and if people think we're favourite, that's great. We'll just go out and try to do what we've done all year and play golf really and

hopefully come out on top, and we'd just like to thank people for supporting us and, hopefully, we can do them proud.'

Q. 'You have the home crowd, the home course, you have the bookies that all expect you to win... Is there any extra pressure on you guys knowing the expectation is there for to you win?'
LLOYD SALTMAN: 'I don't really think so. The players on our team all expect to play well so we are putting pressure on ourselves as it is – even to do well in the practice round.

'So, I don't think anything is going to change other than we want to go out and play well ourselves and then, you know, we probably put more pressure on ourselves than anyone, anyway. If we keep on going, we'll be just fine.'
RORY McILROY: 'Might be a little different for me just because I'm from here. But I think what Lloyd says, we just sort of expect ourselves to play well every week and if we don't, we're not happy.

'I don't think the pressure that we put on ourselves is the only pressure that you should feel, or we do feel. So I think we just go out there, have our own expectations, don't care about what other people think, and go out and play golf and hope we beat the Americans.'

Unfortunately for Rory and the lads, it wasn't to be. Team USA defeated Team GB&I by a score of 12.5 to 11.5 and it wasn't one of Rory's better days at the office – going 1-2-1 in the competition. 'Maybe it was the weight of expectation that got the better of him,' a source commented. 'He was under enormous pressure to produce, especially with all those fans willing him on. It's easy to forget that he was still just an 18-year-old lad at the time. He wasn't an experienced pro – and don't forget that even Padraig Harrington also found it tough going when the expectation on him was similarly as high in the Walker Cup in 1991.'

Certainly there was an undercurrent of sympathy as well as disappointment among the crowd that their local hero hadn't delivered, but they knew he would improve and that his nerves would settle and he would get better and better – after all, that had been the cycle of his development since the early days. He was a player who got better with time, who used experience to propel himself to new levels; he was not someone who delved too deeply in negativity, he knew the best way forward was to accept a setback and move on fast.

The *Daily Telegraph*'s rather appropriately named Mark Reason could see the logic in the idea that expectation had felled Rory: 'Rory McIlroy is not yet up there with George Best in this corner of Northern Ireland. The local hero generously conceded a putt on the 17th hole and then 3-stabbed the last from 20ft to hand his Walker Cup singles match to a shaky Billy Horschel. McIlroy may also have handed the Americans the momentum to retain the cup.

'It is easy to forget that McIlroy is still just 18. Oliver Fisher did phenomenal things in this match two years ago and he was just 16, but Fisher did not have that hag called expectation hanging on his shoulder. McIlroy has been the pin-up boy of this match for two years. It will be almost a relief when he turns pro tomorrow.'

The Walker Cup organisers had completed pen portraits of each of the team members for the GB&I and the US. Their analysis of Rory illustrates the stage he was at in his career as he now prepared for the big jump towards becoming a pro: 'McIlroy underlined his reputation as one of the game's most promising talents in July's Open Championship at Carnoustie where he picked up the Silver Medal. The Irish teenager burst on to the scene in 2005 when, at the age of 16, he became the youngest winner of both the West of Ireland title and the Irish Close Amateur championship. He retained both crowns in 2006 as well as adding the European Amateur championship to his blossoming collection of silverware. A regular in the Irish international set-up, McIlroy made his mark on the European Tour earlier in the year when he made the cut in the Dubai Desert Classic.'

Let's now move on to Rory's pro career, while at the same time looking back over his feats at Carnoustie and Dubai – quite remarkable ones considering, yes, he was still an amateur at that time.

CHAPTER 4

OPENING STATEMENT

It was to be at Carnoustie in 2007 that Rory would really smash his way into the golfing limelight. Aged 18 and still an amateur, he would turn in a performance that would leave the public, the contestants and the media stunned – and transform him into an international golfing star. The prodigy had finally come of age: now there would be few who did not immediately recognise the name of Rory McIlroy.

The boy had always said he was aiming to win Majors, even from those early days when he filled out his own scorecard at Holywood Golf Club. Now he would lay down a marker for the future: 'This is me, this is what I can do and there's a lot more to come. I'm on my way!'

Already he had proved he was doing just that when he played in his first pro tournament at the 2005 British Masters as a 16-year-old and in 2007, when he made his first cut in a professional tournament. It happened at the European Tour's Dubai Desert Classic in early February. Rory opened with back-to-back scores of 69, then shot 71 and 76 on the weekend. He finished tied for 52nd place: at the time, he was 17 years and 10 months old.

Now in Scotland, he was determined to enjoy The Open tournament and to do Ireland proud. This was to be his first Open and he would make the record books by becoming the first amateur from Northern Ireland or Ireland to make an Open cut since Joe Carr in 1965. During practice, Rory was all smiles, talking and shaking hands with spectators, but he put on his serious hat when the action began, knowing this was his moment. He was also realistic enough to know he wasn't going to win the event – there was, after all, the little matter of a world-class pro field headed by the then legendary Woods.

The Tiger was hot favourite with the bookies to land his third consecutive Open title and it would be a brave man who bet against the American as he attempted to become the first player in 50 years to achieve that feat. If he won, Woods would be the first player to do so since Peter Thomson in 1954–56. Jamie Anderson (1877–79) and Bob Ferguson (1880–82) had also won three straight Open titles.

Tiger was confident this was possible although he knew he would need a bit of luck to pull it off and chalk up a 13th Major crown. 'All I know is that I feel good about my preparation so far,' he said in a press conference two days before teeing off. 'I've got one more day to prepare and we'll see how the tournament builds. If I continue doing the things that I'm doing – I like the way I'm swinging, I like the way my short game is, and I like the way my speed is on the greens so far – I just have to carry that into the tournament.'

Woods would play in Group 15, along with Paul Lawrie (who won The Open in 1999) and Justin Rose in the first two rounds, teeing off at 9.10am on the first day. Rory would be the 38th out on the green, with Miguel Angel Jiménez and Henrik Stenson, at 13.45pm.

But Carnoustie had been none too welcoming for Woods at the last Open held there in 1999. Then, he tied for seventh with a 10-over-par 294 but he claimed the previous flop in Scotland didn't worry him and that he actually loved playing on links courses like Carnoustie: 'I grew up on kikuyu grass golf courses and you never would bump and run a golf ball there. I thought it was neat to putt from 40 to 50 yards off the green, hit 5-irons from 135 yards and run the ball because the conditions dictate and it allowed you to do it as well. That to me was fun – I immediately just loved it. I just wish that we could play more golf on it, but you only get one time a year, basically.'

Ernie Els warned Woods and the new youngsters like McIlroy that it would not be easy to crack Carnoustie; that it was one of the most demanding courses in the calendar. He said: 'It's got length. It's got great bunkering – you've really got to have your wits with you to play this golf course. It's probably the best-bunkered course that you'll ever find anywhere in the world. With the weather conditions and the way that the layout is, it's a very demanding layout – you've got to play every shot in the bag. Every links shot you can think of, you get tested here. It's got everything.

'If we have wind like we did on Tuesday morning – conditions like that, or any kind of wind on this golf course – it just becomes a lot more difficult than you think. You really do have to hit the ball well here. The greens are extremely subtle – just like all links courses, they're hard to read.'

So, the scene was set: it would be hard, it would be demanding and Rory would be up against a man determined to blitz the field and fire his way into the record books. But he remained confident and sure of his own ability; he also had an ambition of his own. He wanted to try and emulate Justin Rose who, as a 17-year-old amateur in 1998, pitched in at the last hole in The Open at Royal Birkdale, a shot that claimed him 4th place. And he also wanted to win the silver medal as the best amateur to make the cut.

Certainly, there were shades of Rose's magnificent display as Rory got off to a flier on the first day at Carnoustie, carding a 3-under-68 to command a share of 3rd place. His flawless, bogey-free round meant he was just three shots behind leader Sergio Garcia and one to make up on Paul McGinley. Already he was the favourite to achieve his ambition of claiming the silver. That pleased him, as did the knowledge that he was a stroke ahead of his hero, Woods. Rory said afterwards: 'It's a pretty special feeling, finishing one better than Tiger and also out-shooting my playing partners. I was just trying to learn as much as possible from Miguel Angel Jiménez, who's terrific, and Henrik Stenson, who's won a world golf championship. Coming into the week, I just wanted to try to make the cut and win the silver medal.'

He also felt he was benefiting from a good build-up: 'After the European Team Championships last week, I just went home, relaxed and tried to get my head around playing in The Open. I took a couple of days off and just relaxed, and then I practised Friday and Saturday. And then got here on Sunday and just had – well, two practice rounds, Monday and Tuesday, and then played the loop, the last four last night and Wednesday.

'I played the practise rounds with some pretty good players as well. I played with Trevor Immelman and Niclas Fasth and Richie Ramsay. And I played four holes with Nick Faldo on Monday but it was a bit wet for him, so he went in. I tried to prepare, like any other tournament – just try and go out there, play your own game.'

Rory was also 11 strokes ahead of Nick Faldo, whose videos he had studied while growing up in Holywood, and four ahead of another one of his heroes and mentors: fellow Northern Irishman, Darren Clarke. At the news conference after the first day, Rory added: '[I] pushed both of them, but to play the toughest Open course with no bogeys is pretty good. I played really well out there. I was very nervous the first few holes. But when I birdied the 5th, I got in my stride and got going there, and played some really solid golf and probably should have birdied the 7th as well. But overall this was a really good day – I had been nervous at first, but then soaked up the atmosphere and really enjoyed it.'

And he thanked his supporters for helping him keep his cool that first day at Carnoustie: 'It was just like a chill down the back of my spine with the ovation I got, it's fantastic! Holywood Golf Club are just so supportive of me – it's great to see so many people over. I think with their support it's really helped me, not just today but throughout the year to get me where I am now. They've just been fantastic.'

At the press conference he was asked if he would be able to sleep that night, given Woods was breathing right down his neck, to which he replied: 'Yes, I think I'll be able to sleep all right. I'm knackered. But it's just – yeah, it's a pretty special feeling to say you shot one better than Tiger. And then to be playing partners as well, with Henrik and Miguel, it's just awesome. Yeah, I'll probably go home tonight and put my feet up, watch the highlights and then probably just go straight to bed. I've got a pretty early start in the morning – I don't think I'll have any trouble sleeping tonight.'

He added that Woods remained his hero and point-of-excellence reference: 'From an early age Tiger Woods has always been my hero – like, he won the '96 US Amateur and I think after that it was just Tiger, Tiger, Tiger. And he's been my one big influence in my whole golfing life.'

Rory was also asked about his personal life – what he liked to do, and about when he had left school and with how many GCSEs. Laughing, he answered the throng of awe-struck hacks: 'A few [GCSEs]. I just started playing full-time amateur golf. The golf [authorities] in Ireland have been supportive – they've helped me tremendously and I've travelled all over the world at their expense, pretty much.

And it's great to have that support behind you. I'm pretty much a normal teenager. I like to go out and go to the cinema, try and think about golf as little as possible when I'm off the golf course and just try and lead a normal life. I think I've pretty much done that for the last 18 years. I'm a normal teenager, but I'm a pretty good golfer as well.'

There was no doubt about that last statement as he was proving beyond all measure at his first Open – although his caddie would claim he could have done even better in the first round! 'He probably left a couple of shots out there,' Gordon Faulkner told BBC Sport, 'but it won't bother him too much – his temperament is that good. He's about 15 years ahead of where he should be when it comes to the mental side of golf.'

Meanwhile, his parents were simply delighted that their boy had done so magnificently. 'It was an incredible day,' said Rosie McIlroy. 'Totally above all of our expectations.' Although dad Gerry said he wasn't so surprised as his boy had 'been playing really well of late.'

After his first-round exploits, Rory did indeed sleep well and was back on the green bright and fresh the next day. This time, it would not be quite so eye-opening a round, but still impressive: he slipped back down the field after a 5-over-par 76, bogeying the 2nd and dropping three more shots before birdies at the 12th and 14th put him back in business.

Later, he was a little bruised but still proud of his efforts (a 2-over-144), saying: 'To be sitting at plus four isn't too bad. If I can go out and shoot a score like Chris DiMarco did, the Top 10 is well within my reach. I want to play in this next year and the easiest way to do that is to finish in the Top 10.'

And the really good news was that as the only one of the field's six amateurs to make the cut, Rory was now guaranteed the silver medal he so craved. 'I just wanted to go out there and try my best, play golf and enjoy it – and that is what I did today,' he explained afterwards. 'I didn't get upset with bad shots.'

Once again he paid tribute to the fans cheering him on and encouraging him at every hole. 'The interest has been pretty big,' he admitted. 'There were a lot of TV cameras following me and it was nice to play in front of crowds like that. I wasn't too nervous today – I was probably more pumped up than nervous.'

In Saturday's third round Rory continued his solid form, going round in a 2-over-par 73. He said he was pleased with his day's work and was now looking forward to the final round on the Sunday – and being presented with the silver medal.

It would prove a day of double celebration as his friend and fellow Irishman Padraig Harrington lifted the trophy after a playoff with Sergio Garcia.

Both players made errors on the 18th as Harrington hit a double-bogey 6 and Garcia followed him with a bogey. With the scores tied at 7-under, the pair went into a four-hole playoff. Harrington went two shots clear at the first hole after Garcia landed his second shot in the bunker. They then parred the next two holes before Harrington went on to win by one shot. Harrington said: 'It's obviously too good –

it's a lot to take in. I tried not to get ahead of myself but it's all coming in now.

'I think if I'd lost it would have been very hard to take, but I didn't allow myself to get down about taking six at the last. But I convinced myself all along I was going to win and that if it was a playoff, I could win that.'

Argentina's Andres Romero finished third on 6-under after he holed 10 birdies on his way to a 4-under-par final round of 67.

And Rory? Well, he finished with a final round of 72, for a 5-over-par total of 289, which placed him tied 42nd on the final leaderboard. A highly creditable end to his first Major – one he had challenged for, let's not forget, while still an amateur. He was 'overjoyed' when presented with the silver medal but admitted to friends that he felt 'a bit knackered' emotionally, physically and mentally after his exertions, telling them he now planned to take a well-deserved holiday in Dubai. 'It's been a pretty draining week for me, obviously, with all the attention,' he conceded. 'It's more mentally out there, because you have to hit a good shot all the time. It's difficult to do that for 72 holes, and early starts and getting home late and stuff, but it's been great and I've really enjoyed it.'

On the night itself, however, he was all for a local celebration in Scotland: 'I might go out into Dundee. I've got a few of my friends that are staying over there this week, so I might go out for a while tonight.'

At the press conference after proceedings had been wrapped up, he also revealed a little more on his thoughts about his first Open. He started off by admitting that winning the silver medal had made it all worthwhile even though he was disappointed not to finish in the Top 10: 'That [the silver medal] was my goal at the start of the week and then after my good first round, I said to myself to just finish in the Top 10. But I obviously didn't do that. But overall I'm really happy – to end the week with a birdie on the last was pretty special.

'Hopefully it's the shape of things to come. I think I'm getting better all the time, progressing as a player. Hopefully I've got a few more Open championships in me. I think it's a great performance – first Major, first Open championship – and hopefully, I can go on to bigger and better things.'

Asked if he would change his approach work to hitting the ball (which several analysts had commented on) and maybe slow it down a little, he said: 'I've always been quick and that's just the way I play. I just think – I stand up, look at the shot, assess it, know the shot I'm going to hit, and I hit it. I don't mess about. I think my short routine is OK. I have a couple of practice swings, visualise the shot, feel it, see it and do it, and let it go. That's pretty much the easiest way to play for me. There's no point in taking time over things because you just confuse yourself so I stand up, look at the target and hit it. That's the way I've always been.'

Finally, did he think he could one day win The Open?

He smiled and nodded towards the players out on the green, who were still continuing their final round, including the then leader Sergio Garcia. Rory said: 'Sergio is out there at the minute and he's played in an Open as an amateur before. And look where he is now: he's leading The Open championship. And he was in the last group last year, and he's had a lot of good performances. So if I can progress over the next few years and keep improving, I certainly think I can be contending for an Open – hopefully in the near future.'

Certainly he was now not the only one of that opinion. Analysts, fans and fellow players around the world all nodded in agreement. Respected golf writer Gary Van Sickle of *Sports Illustrated* made the point that not only had Rory made his mark – he had made his mark as someone whose name could even be muttered in the same whispered tones of reverence as Tiger Woods', given the similarities in determination and early success at The Open: 'The crowd was thick around the practice green at Carnoustie last Saturday morning, which should've been a tipoff that something was up. Yet Rory McIlroy of Northern Ireland, a slight 18-year-old whose freckled, cherubic cheeks make him look more like 14, eased past a pair of security guards and onto the practice area with the confidence of a veteran pro, dropped a couple of balls, then casually began stroking putts toward a cup near the one being used by Tiger Woods.

'There was no exchange of pleasantries, eye contact or backward glances by Woods, who was hard at work in his office and apparently didn't notice the pride of Holywood, a town of about 12,000 near Belfast. That made Tiger about the only person at the British Open to miss McIlroy, who would finish 42nd (with a 5-over-289) to win the silver medal as low amateur, an award claimed by Woods in 1996.'

Now Rory would turn pro and aim even higher. And the stars of golf had been warned: there's a new kid in town and he is a genius.

CHAPTER 5

TURNING PRO

On 19 September 2007, Rory finally waved goodbye to his days as an amateur and turned professional. He signed with International Sports Management, entrusting his future to the top agent Andrew 'Chubby' Chandler. It was a wise move – the youngster could now get on with playing and perfecting his golf while leaving all the outside interest decisions to Chubby, who had already shown he had what it takes in guiding the topsy-turvy career of Rory's compatriot and friend, Darren Clarke.

In a more recent piece the respected *Sports History* outlined how Rory had chosen well in Chandler, calling him 'the hottest agent' and summing up his style of doing business and reputation in this way: 'If you walk into a clubhouse lounge at any of your better golf tournaments these days, anywhere in the world, there's a chance you're going to smell the player agent Andrew (Chubby) Chandler. Chandler is partial to a cologne called Jo Malone which he slaps on, Chandler says in his particular and broad accent, "about three times the usual dose." Salesmen – even an Englishman selling rare golf talent – often find it useful to stand out, or at least that's how Chandler feels about it.

'Chandler, 58, from Bolton, is selling an excellent line. He's the founder and managing director of a company called International Sports Management (ISM), which represents the South African Ernie Els, the Englishman Lee Westwood, the Irishman Rory McIlroy, the Indian Jeev Milka Singh, the Californian Christina Kim and a bunch of others you've heard of or most likely will. The company, with 30 employees, represents about 40 golfers, 25 soccer players, 10 cricketers and one Paralympic swimmer.'

With the reassurance of larger-than-life Chubby now by his side, Rory could enter events confidently. His first pro tournament was to be the British Masters and he would talk about his trust in Chandler and Clarke at the press conference on the first day of the event: 'Everyone knows that I have known Darren and Chubby for quite a while now and it was the perfect move for me to come out from a pretty good amateur career and turn pro, especially at this event because ISM are running the show here.

'I am really pleased how things have gone over the last few years as an amateur and hope to carry on from there. As for my expectations for this week, I just want to go out and enjoy myself in my first event as a pro. I have a number of events to try and get my card and if that doesn't happen, I have Tour School as well. I am not putting too much pressure on myself but I would love to go out this week and play well.

'I met Darren on my ninth birthday at Portrush and have known him since then through the Darren Clarke Foundation. The next time I met him, I was 12 and since then we have had a great relationship. He gave me his phone number when I was 13 or 14 and he has been fantastic to me. Anything I wanted to know, I could always ring him up and ask him, and it was great to have that. Every time I play in a professional event, I try and get a practice round with Darren as he knows so much and there is so much you can learn from Darren. I enjoyed nine holes with him today [in a practice session].'

When asked for a final overview of his amateur career and to pinpoint who he was particularly grateful for help, he said: 'The Golfing Union of Ireland, first of all. I have travelled all over the world at their expense and they have been fantastic. I have played for them all over the world, in South Africa for the European nations trophy.

'The relationship with Darren – he has been a big influence and always on the other end of the phone. Mum and Dad obviously have been pivotal in my career and have made a lot of sacrifices for me. They have worked very hard to get me where they have and I think this is the point where they step back and let me get on with it. There are too many people to thank (but I think they all know who they are), who have helped me get to this point.'

Meanwhile, Chubby had told the press how he rated his boy Rory right up there with Tiger Woods and Sergio Garcia as one of the most exciting prospects he had ever seen. Rory said that he felt honoured by such an association: 'It is nice to be mentioned in the same breath as Sergio and Tiger and if I can make a start like they did in their professional career, I will be very happy. I am just going to go and try my hardest, and try and play good golf, and hopefully the results will follow.'

So, how did it differ to play in pro tournaments than amateur – judging from his experiences gained while playing in a few as an amateur? 'Playing as an amateur in professional events is quite different but playing as a professional in a professional event is different as every shot counts and one shot could cost you £20,000 or whatever.

'The courses are set up tougher. This week, the long rough is eight or ten yards off the greens but other courses it has been two or three yards and around the greens is where it is tougher in championship venues. If you miss the green, you have to work harder to save par.

'Every time you go out on Tour, you feel more comfortable; you get to know more people. It has been great as all the guys have made me feel welcome out here. Because I have that experience hopefully the transition won't be as difficult for me as it has been for some guys in the past.'

Certainly, he was no novice in terms of sponsorship. Thanks to his own meteoric rise and the efforts of Chubby, he was already doing well. He explained that he had a host of backers, starting with the Jumeirah Group, the Dubai-based luxury hotel company who had backed him immediately he turned pro – in no small part because their chief financial officer, Alaister Murray, came from Rory's hometown of Holywood and loved the promise he saw in the youngster. Rory admitted as much when he mentioned Jumeirah at the top of his list of sponsors, saying: 'I played in the Dubai Desert Classic the last couple of years and have a relationship with them, which is great. The chief financial officer is actually from my hometown of Hollywood so that is where it started.

'It is a great relationship for me to have as Jumeirah are expanding all the time and they are going to have hotels all over the world and as I hopefully grow as a professional golfer, they will grow as a brand and I think that is a perfect combination.'

His clubs were sponsored by Titleist, which also pleased him: 'That is another good sponsor. I have played Titleist all my life and it was great they wanted me as a staff player. That works out well as I don't want to be changing clubs and tinkering with things as I start out as a professional.'

Backing from Footjoy for his shoes and a couple of sponsors in Ireland – Bennett Construction and private equity investment firm FL Partners – completed Rory's early deals and provided him with the necessary stability as he now concentrated on the greens.

So, just how did he rate his prospects in the British Masters? 'I am hitting it well and the greens are so good if you are rolling the ball well that you have a lot of chances. I think this course suits me and I am driving it well – if I can get a few putts to drop, I will hopefully have a good shout.

'The greens are a lot quicker than last week. I was thinking about changing putter but have the light one in the bag, which is good for these fast greens and I putted well this morning, so I will keep that in the bag.'

Rory did well on his first pro round – finishing on a bogey-free 3-under-par 69. He declared himself 'well pleased' and added: 'I opened up with a couple of pars. Chipped in on the 11th – which was nice – and then chipped in on 12 for birdie. Settled the nerves a bit. A 69 is a good score today; there's a lot of crosswinds so it's quite tough to hold fairways. You're always hitting the ball across them, so it was quite difficult but I gave myself a lot of chances out there. I could have been a bit better if I had holed a few putts but 69, I'll take it going into tomorrow.'

When asked at the press conference how he felt after his first round as a professional, he said 'it was OK' and that he 'wasn't really as nervous' as he was at The Open. He added: 'I just went out and played. I just said, go out and play the same way I did last week at the Oxfordshire. I just went out, strolled around and hit a few good shots, holed a few putts and that's all I did today. Just strolled round, gave myself a lot of chances and figure if I can keep doing that for the rest of the week, I'll be very happy.'

Did he feel nervous as he teed off? 'I didn't really think about it, to be honest. You always get butterflies on the first tee but I definitely wasn't as nervous as I was at The Open or the Walker Cup. It doesn't feel any different at the minute

– professional, amateur, it's still the same game. I didn't really think about it too much.'

And what of his parents, proudly watching their son take his first strides as a pro on the circuit? 'Mum probably was [nervous]. Dad's all right. He doesn't care – well, he cares but it doesn't matter to him if I shoot 69 or 79. He's just happy that I'm playing golf. I think he's happy that I've got all the right people around me as well. So, after this week, Mum and Dad aren't going to come to that many tournaments. I think Dad's happy with the situation I'm in, and he trusts the people that are around me to take care of me and sort of help me along this new path.'

On the Friday, Rory shot 78 in the second round of his pro debut and made the cut. He declared himself happy to have made the cut but was not so pleased about the rest of his round: 'The way I finished was not good. I rushed my tee shot and hooked it in the water. Hit a great fourth shot in and hit a pretty good putt. I knew two putts would be enough and after a bad start to the back nine, that was good.

'I played well in the first 10 holes and then hit it in that bunker again on 11, had to play out sideways and shot 6. I am not trying to say I have been unlucky but I have not had any good breaks. Every bunker I have been up against the lip and not been able to hit more than 50 yards. Hopefully my luck will turn a bit over the weekend and I can shoot a couple of rounds in the 60s and get myself up the leaderboard again. Saturday is moving day and if I can get some good weather, I am hitting well, there is no reason I can't go out and shoot in the mid-60s. I always expected to make the cut, so happy to make the cut and hopefully I can improve on it over the weekend.'

On the Saturday he was in better form, going round in 70. He told the gathered press corps, he was 'very pleased' to have improved on his Friday showing, though disappointed to have finished with a dropped shot on the last hole. Rory said: 'It is not my favourite hole on the course, the 18th. I really don't like the drive and just bailed out on it. I hit a really good shot with my 2nd, then just hit my putt a bit hard and overread the par putt. Overall I am very pleased. Shot 70 this morning and it will move me up the field a little. Hopefully, it will give me an extra hour in bed!

'But I'm disappointed to have fallen back [over the three days]. I never came here with the mindset it was good to make the cut. I came here wanting to do my best and if I can do that, I know I am good enough to contend out here.'

He was even more disappointed when he fell back further still on the final round on the Sunday, hitting a 73, which left him on a 2-over-par total of 290. At the end of his first tournament as a professional, Rory McIlroy had tied for 42nd place. He had entered the Brit Masters with high hopes and while he left with those hopes dashed, he had also learned some important lessons and picked up invaluable experience. Afterwards, he tempered his disappointment and was much more philosophical about the outcome, saying: 'It could have been a lot worse, after the five bogeys going out [on his final round]. But I made a good swing on 10 and hit every green coming in, apart from 18, and could have had six birdies. I'm playing well, hitting it really nicely, but I guess I didn't really hole enough putts this week. I holed some good six-footers, but didn't really give myself a lot of birdie chances. From 15 feet, I hit a lot of good putts that didn't go in. Hopefully they will at the Dunhill [his next scheduled tournament]. My first event as a professional has gone well, better than most. I'd give myself a B-minus for the week. There's room for improvement, as there always is.'

This honest appraisal was typical of the boy and his continued development. And it was why he was on the way to becoming a certain great: he never got too excited or off-track when he did exceptionally well and never went too low when things didn't turn out as well as he hoped. For someone so young, he was a balanced individual with good self-awareness but that didn't stop him from admitting that he enjoyed the adulation of the crowd, who had lapped up his first pro show on the circuit! And he also liked the cash he had earned for the event and had plans on how he would spend it. He admitted: 'Yes, I've enjoyed the attention and signing autographs as a professional. I can give stuff away now too, now I'm getting it free! It's been absolutely fantastic and everyone has looked after me ever so well. I was expecting there to be a lot of interest in me after The Open and Walker Cup, and with me turning pro at a big event like this – I think I've dealt with it pretty well.

'I've got a nice little pay-cheque of about £10–12,000, which is a nice start. What will I spend it on? I may take Holly [his girlfriend] to the cinema but I'm actually going to be looking for a house next week. I'm going to move out, but I'm looking in Holywood because I want to be near enough to Mum so that she can still do my washing for me!'

Rory would now take a short break – to regroup and analyse what he had done right and where he had struggled – before the next event, the Dunhill Links. After the pressure and inevitable goldfish bowl-like attention that had accompanied his first pro appearance, he looked forward to relaxing with his family and unwinding a little. He said: 'I shall have a nice little break this week to recuperate before going to Scotland to have a good go at the Dunhill Links. Playing here this week has been good preparation for that. There may be some more woolly hats needed, though – but I love links and I'm looking forward to it.

'Before then, I'm playing with my dad against Darren Clarke and his dad Godfrey tomorrow in an exhibition match at Darren's new course in Sligo. It should be good. My dad says he hasn't been playing for two years but he's been practising a lot. He played four times last week. He's off two, Darren's dad is off six, so Darren and I should just leave them to it, I think!'

But it was to take him a while to adjust to the demands of life as a pro. Golf analyst Michael Fitzpatrick would best sum up the wonderboy's standing in 2007, cleverly making the valid comparison between his somewhat stuttering start to that previously of Justin Rose: 'McIlroy's decision to turn pro was scrutinised by the European press and many European tour pros. The second McIlroy relinquished his amateur status, the comparisons to Justin Rose began running rampant. Similar to McIlroy, Rose turned pro shortly after an outstanding performance as an amateur at the British Open. At the 1998 Open, the then 17-year-old Rose holed a miraculous shot on the 72nd hole from 40 yards out to finish in a tie for fourth. Upon turning pro the week after his fourth-place finish at the British Open, Rose went on to miss 21 straight cuts on the European Tour.

'Rose, now ranked 15th in the world, has obviously turned into an exceptional tour professional. However, it was clear from the beginning that Rose was not quite ready for the pro circuit back in 1998, and many thought McIlroy would follow a very similar path. McIlroy did indeed get off to a fairly slow start to his professional career. In 2007 he finished 95th on the European Tour's Order of Merit.'

But Rory was to make an impact in his second and third tournaments as a pro – indeed, such an impact that he would become the youngest and quickest affiliate member of the European Tour to secure his card.

CHAPTER 6

CARDS ON
THE TABLE

Rory was thrilled when he earned his European Tour Card in October 2007. He had planned to hit the pro circuit hard and fast but even he was surprised at just how quickly success would come in his career – only his second and third tournaments, to be exact. After finishing tied 42nd in the British Masters, he had headed up to Scotland for the Dunhill Links, pleased but knowing he had much more to offer.

He knew the analysts, the public and his fellow pros were all watching him with eager eyes to assess whether he did indeed have what it takes or whether he would follow in the footsteps of the aforementioned Justin Rose, who had taken some time – and considerable effort – to emerge as a contender after turning pro himself.

As Rory arrived at St Andrews at the start of October, he knew that he would have his work cut out to make a big impression against a top-notch field. He would be up against defending champion Padraig Harrington, who was looking to win the event for a record-breaking third time. Harrington, of course, had also won The Open three months earlier at Carnoustie and would provide stiff competition for Rory and the other hopefuls aiming to crack the event at three of the world's greatest links courses in the Old Course at St Andrews, Carnoustie and Kingsbarns.

Rory also knew that victory at the Dunhill was often a welcome catalyst for great things to follow. Twelve months earlier, Harrington had used his second Dunhill Links title as a stepping-stone on the way to winning his first European Tour Order of Merit crown. And he had also laid claim to becoming the first Irishman in 25 years to win the Irish Open and then added the 137th Open to his list of honours.

Rory would do well to see off the challenge of Harrington, the only player to win the Dunhill Links twice; he would also face other class acts, including further former winners of the event – Paul Lawrie (2001), Stephen Gallacher (2004), Colin Montgomerie (2005) and Lee Westwood, who had lifted the trophy in 2003 and was arriving on the back of winning the British Masters.

Rory dreamed of winning the event but was realistic enough to know even a Top 10 finish would be an achievement. And he would do better than that – much better, finishing third and virtually guaranteeing he would earn that much-coveted Tour card. He shot 71-67-67-68 to finish at 15-under 273.

England's Nick Dougherty claimed his second title on The European Tour, carding a final-round 1-under-par 71 for an 18-under-par total of 270, which put him two ahead of Justin Rose. But Rory was also the talk of the town as he edged closer to becoming the youngest Affiliate Member in the history of the European Tour ever to earn the coveted Tour card.

When he later explained what the result meant to him he was beaming like a Cheshire cat, at the same time revealing that Westwood had really given him a boost by telling him he was already good enough to win the event! 'I knew at the start of the week I needed to do something pretty special to get my Tour card and I am absolutely ecstatic. There have been a lot of great players come into the game pretty young, obviously Tiger [Woods] and Sergio [Garcia], and I'm trying to take it all in my stride. When I talked about my chances of making the card this week to Lee, he told me I could win the tournament. When someone like Lee tells you that, it gives you a lot of confidence. Hopefully this is a huge step for bigger and better things.'

Rory listened intently as winner Dougherty explained how the result would now change his life, at the age of 25. His words would give the youngster hope and make him even more determined that he, too, would start to win events soon and experience the same seismic change the more experienced player talked about. Dougherty would also make the valid point that winning does take time and effort and practice – and sometimes you need to be patient as you travel along the road towards it. For the young man from Northern Ireland, those were wise words indeed and invaluable advice. Dougherty said: 'Obviously I'm delighted to win, but more especially in the manner that I did it. The start I had felt like a similar start to other tournaments where I had other chances to win but you know, I spoke to my dad before I went out and I felt very nervous, to be honest. It means so much, you know, to win and as much as I really wanted for it not to mean that much to me, it's difficult. You know, it's my nature to care that much – I just felt it was in my hands.

'And it's a life-changing win in that what it's done. It's changed the perspective of this year; it's changed obviously where I am in the world, where I am with my own personal goals in my career and what I've done. It's just so hard for me to go through the process without me jumping and wanting to get to the end too quickly.

'I've done fantastically well this year. It's because of what I've done that I was in a position to be able to win this week. The way I dealt with the start today – I didn't have those attributes, you know, 10 months ago – and I think I've learned from the errors. And thankfully the errors have been in events that haven't been as important as this one and so it's nice for me to get it right in the right place.'

Third place would also boost Rory's bank balance – to the tune of €211,000, to be exact. He could now add it to the €12,000 pocketed for his showing at the British Masters. It seemed this pro game was a walk in the park for Rory – his transition from amateur had been so smooth. After the last round he would be asked at the press conference whether he was surprised that it had been so easy to bridge the gap to pro. In response, he said: 'Not really. I think because I've played so many events as an amateur in professional tournaments, I think I've fitted in really well and I know most of the guys out here, anyway. So, that's been pretty nice. You know, if I can keep going the way I am, there's a lot of good things out on Tour for me. So, hopefully I can just keep playing well.'

However, he admitted that it 'had been a pretty nice feeling' to have finished in the top three, adding: 'At the start of the week, I knew that I had to do something pretty special to try and get my Tour card.'

He was asked if, as he worked through his final round, he was aware that third place would almost guarantee his Tour card. 'Not really,' he replied. 'I went to 15-under after the 10th, I sort of thought, you know, try and hang on a bit.

'Then I bogeyed 12 and doubled 14, which wasn't so good but I came back really well. I'm really happy, and if I have to go another week until I get my Tour card, I'm happy enough for that. But [the] good thing for that is I probably won't have to go to second stage of Tour School now – I'm straight into the final even if I don't play well the next couple of weeks.'

So, what was his overall view of one of his most encouraging displays ever – and this would presumably be a day he would forever savour? 'Yeah, it's been absolutely fantastic,' he declared. 'To finish in the top five at this event is something pretty special and it's obviously my best-ever performance in a professional event and to do it here at St Andrews as well is pretty good. So, overall I'm just really happy and you know, we'll see how the guys finish on the course and hopefully, somehow I might be able to get my card.

'St Andrews is always a course I've played well at, and I knew if I could go out and play the front nine in 32, 33, which I did, I would do OK. I think the par 5s cost me. I played those at 3-over today, which wasn't so good but I'm not going to complain because I've played so well – I'm just really happy and hopefully it's a huge step for bigger and better things.'

And it was. Just a week later he would secure his Tour card by finishing tied fourth – another remarkable result for a boy who had just joined the pro circuit – at the Madrid Open. Rory shot a 1-over-par 73 in the first round but had moved to 3-under by the end of the Friday after a fine 68. He went two strokes better on the Saturday with a 66 – and then carded a 70 on the final day to finish with a 277 total and that excellent 4th place.

Denmark's Mads Vibe-Hastrup claimed his first European Tour title, carding a closing 67 with six birdies and just one bogey. He finished three ahead of Spain's Alejandro Cañizares, with Daniel Vancsik of Argentina claiming 3rd.

Rory was tied 4th with France's Gregory Bourdy – and the youngster admitted he had nearly been biting his nails as he struggled for consistency in that final-round 70, which included an eagle, five birdies and five bogeys. He said afterwards: 'I would have taken 4th when I came here. I think I've done very well after all that has gone on over the last few weeks and I hope to follow it on next week [in Portugal]. I am playing very well at the moment – I am hitting it really well. If I could get a couple more putts to drop, it would make the difference.'

Certainly the fans believed he was at the start of something big. One, Andy Brown, observed: 'A lot of people seem to believe this young man has a very bright future ahead of him and he has already made an impression on the people who keenly follow the game. A tie for 3rd at the Dunhill Links and then at tied for 4th at the Madrid Open ensured that he secured his card for the 2008 season, which has made him the youngest Affiliate member on the European Tour to turn pro. He was even invited for last week's Target World Challenge but he had to decline that invitation because of his schedule.

'This lad, who has just turned 18, will be in sharp focus during the 2008 season and everyone will be interested in his progress. There are many who believe Nick Faldo would be hard-pressed to ignore him for the Ryder Cup. While it looks like a longshot, if he makes it, one can't think of a better boost for someone's fledgling career. He has already had a decent finish in The Open and after having missed his first cut in his professional career in Hong Kong, he seems more determined to perform at the highest level. One can only wish him all the best.'

Another Brown – Dave, a lifelong golf fan – was a little more wary of 'going overboard' about Rory. He said: 'Sure, he looks a great prospect but let's remember the dip Justin

Rose suffered after turning pro and let's give Rory a bit of breathing space. It's easy to forget he's still a young lad – if we put him under too much pressure, if we create too much expectation, he might suffer, too. Let him develop at his own pace – he's doing fine and will do even better when he's got a bit more experience under his belt.'

Whatever your opinion at the time, one thing was for sure: Rory McIlroy was creating opinions and demanding attention. He was making headlines for all the right reasons – his golfing ability and enjoying early success after turning pro. By the end of the 2007 European Tour season, he had netted €277,255 and finished in 95th place on the Order of Merit list. He was the highest ranked associate member and felt optimistic and confident about 2008, believing this could be the year he brought home his first trophy on the pro circuit. The boy wonder was convinced he was on the verge of something big, bolstered by those great results in Scotland and Madrid.

CHAPTER 7

LOVE AND EIGHT

By the end of 2008 Rory had roared up the rankings – from 95th to 36th – and earned €400,000 more than the previous year (although of course he only turned pro in the September of 2007). He had also made it into the Top 100 world rankings. Before the start of the 2008 Euro Tour season, in December 2007, he made his growing presence felt on the circuit by snubbing Tiger Woods! The US legend had asked him to play in the Target World Challenge but Rory turned him down, saying, 'I was thrilled that they would want to invite me considering I'm only just starting out on my career, but the event clashes with the European Open and that's an event I would be stupid not to play.'

He began his 2008 season proper at the Hong Kong Open but this would prove a real disappointment as he failed to make the cut for the first time as a pro, missing it by four strokes. In the first round, he shot a 69 but slipped up in the second, carding a 74.

He was down, though not too depressed. A week later, he finished in a tie for 15th at the MasterCard Masters in Australia but it would be a topsy-turvy season with another 9 cuts missed and only by the second half of the year had he truly started to hit the form expected of him after his fine showings in Madrid and Scotland of the previous year.

The one highlight of the early part of the season was his display at the Irish Open in the middle of May, where he finished 7th with signs of his form returning. Rory contributed rounds of 70, 72, 70 and 70 – for a 282 total and a useful cheque of €75,000 – at the Adare Manor. Before play on the first day, he admitted how much he had been anticipating the event – his first Irish Open as a professional. 'Yeah, I'm looking forward to it,' he told reporters. 'Obviously this is my first time in the Irish Open as a professional. I played in 2005 as an amateur at Carton House. I played this morning and the golf course is really nice and the greens are rolling really well. I think they have set it up quite fairly as well. I don't think the rough is as penal as it was last year, so the scores should be a little better this year.'

He also admitted the weight of expectation had been on his shoulders but that he felt he had coped well so far: 'I'm just trying to do my own thing and keep in control what I can keep control of, and that's all I can do. I think going out last year and getting my Tour card so quickly probably put a lot of expectation on my shoulders but after I played Dubai and took a few weeks off and I came back and played Malaysia and Korea, missed a couple of cuts there, I realised that you can't really get complacent. You just have to keep working hard because all the other guys are working hard out here to try and beat you. I've learned a few things this season and hopefully that will stand me in good stead for the months ahead.'

And it seemed the old-timers had not had their noses put out of joint by him being the new, extremely young kid on the block – in fact, they had gone out of their way to make him feel at home: 'They've been very friendly and open to play practice rounds with me – everyone has made me feel quite comfortable on Tour. I haven't really had any problems or anything. Everyone's been great, especially all of the Irish guys and all of the guys from ISM have been looking after me well. It's been a great learning experience and I would rather be out here than at university, starting my first year.'

So, how did it feel to be playing in Ireland – and wasn't it about time the North got to host The Open? He said: 'I feel wherever it's played in Ireland, it's going to be my home event but obviously it would be great to see it go up North. But I think there's a lot of courses down around Dublin – you have K Club and Carton House, you've got Adare Manor here, and Portmarnock and other courses that can handle big crowds that the Irish Open usually gets. And I don't know if there's any courses in the North with the infrastructure set in place that could handle the amount of people you would get: you don't just have the golfers and the caddies – you've got the media, you've got the spectators and you've got everyone involved in the tournament. It would be great to see it up North, but I don't see it in the foreseeable future.'

Rory declared he was 'satisfied' with his first-round 70 – it was something he could hopefully build on and showed that he had prepared well. 'It's a solid round – I didn't do much wrong today,' he said. 'I hit it really nicely. Gave myself a lot of opportunities, which is great around this golf course. Hopefully I can build on it for the next three days.

'[After] a long couple of weeks over in the Far East, I got home and sort of recharged the batteries a little bit and did a lot of good practice, and it has paid off going into this week. I feel comfortable with my ball striking and I've sharpened up my short game which is good, and overall I feel like I'm playing quite nicely. As I said, if I can play like that for the next three days, I won't be far off.

'I do feel a lot more comfortable in Europe than I do in the Far East and it shows. I played Spain and Portugal in April and I played pretty well there.'

He was still happy after his second round, even though he only carded a 72. 'I played nicely today,' he said. 'Sort of struggled early on, but was 3-over after three. And then the last 15 holes I played in 3-under, which is really good out there today. At least I finished the round well with the 4 on the last and hopefully that will give me a bit of positive energy going into the weekend.

'I'm only 4 off the lead, which I'm quite surprised at. With not much wind, I thought the guys would have kicked on a bit but I'm happy to be where I am and in a good position for the weekend. Hopefully I can play well tomorrow and get myself in contention, and I'll be very happy.'

That was still the case after the Saturday when he hit a second 70, which left him 4-under-par to go with Thursday's. He was still in with a chance and said: 'I've probably played a little better than what the score reflected today but overall, I'm still in there with a chance so I'm pretty pleased. I'm only 4 shots off the lead.'

He was disappointed with certain aspects of his day's work, though: 'I just didn't hole enough putts again. I putted quite well but just from maybe 12, 15 feet; I gave myself a lot of opportunities and didn't really take many. Apart from that, the ball striking is pretty good, a couple of shots here and there but that's always expected. A bit of practice on the putting green tonight and hopefully I can go out and hole those putts tomorrow.'

But Rory would not chalk up that first win as a pro. Instead, Yorkshireman Richard Finch was the surprise winner. Finch shot a 2-under 70 after falling into a river on the last hole to win by two strokes for his second European Tour victory of the season. The 30-year-old, whose first career victory was in the New Zealand Open the previous December, finished at 10-under 278.

At least Finch could see the funny side of it all. 'I never gave a thought to falling in,' he said. 'The momentum on the follow-through took me in. It wasn't that cold – and I was a good swimmer in my youth!'

Felipe Aguilar of Chile took second place at 280 with a closing 70. Gary Murphy shot a 69 to finish another shot back in a tie for 3rd with Maarten Lafeber (67), Robert Karlsson (71) and Lee Westwood (72). Next up was Rory – and he was not too downhearted with his top-five finish. His form had, after all, been a big improvement on his early season displays. 'I came into this week knowing I was playing pretty nicely and I just played really solid,' he observed. 'It's a golf course that suits me. I play better on difficult golf courses where the scoring isn't too low and I just played really nicely. Probably looking back on it tomorrow night, I'll be very happy with the way I finished.

'It's been very good, my first Irish Open as a pro, and to come here with all the expectation on my shoulders, it was absolutely fantastic. The support I got out there was great and I was very pleased with the way I bounced back after my pretty poor start today.

'There are a lot of positives. I played really well. Just looking back over the week, I probably didn't hole my fair share and I gave myself a lot of chances going into that back 9 today. I gave myself a good chance on 15, just pushed the putt, and 16 and 17 hit good chips, and I thought the one on 16 was in.

'I was a bit disappointed with my drive on the last. It was the first time I had missed that fairway on 18 and I thought maybe I could get myself on the fairway and hit one onto the green again, and give myself an eagle chance but a birdie will have to do.'

He left Ireland with his hopes and optimism higher than for some time. A month later, he admitted to reporters to being a little puzzled by his inconsistent form – which included failing to qualify for The Open – but added that he was still enjoying his first full season as a pro, saying: 'I have really enjoyed myself and while it has been a bit up and down, I feel like I am hitting the ball pretty well. It would be nice to have a good second half of the season and I have set myself the goal of playing in the event at Valderrama at the end of the year. A Top 60 Order of Merit finish would be a good way to start my career. I would also like to get into the world's Top 100 in order to get an invitation to the US PGA tournament and hopefully both those goals are still achievable.'

'I played well at the Irish Open and have had a couple of quite steady finishes but haven't been able to be in contention on the final day and that is what I'm really looking to do.'

That ambition would be realised in September 2008 when he made a sustained effort to win his first pro title at the European Masters. He hit a 5-under-par 66 on the Saturday to take a four-shot lead into the final round. Rory was on 13-under-par, four ahead of a group of six, including Robert Dinwiddie (64), Alejandro Cañizares (69) Christian Cevaer (65) and Jean-François Lucquin (69). He was aiming to become the third-youngest to win on tour behind South African Dale Hayes – the youngest – and Seve Ballesteros.

On the opening day, Rory had raced to the top of the leaderboard at Crans-sur-Sierre with a brilliant 63, the lowest score of his pro career and just a stroke off the course record. It meant he would enter the second round three shots ahead of Welsh duo Garry Houston and Kyron Sullivan, plus Argentina's Julio Zapata.

After that first day, he admitted: 'This has been a long time coming for me as I have struggled over the last few months but a score like this really boosts your confidence. Hopefully I can kick on from here and keep on doing what I am doing. I have been hitting the ball well in recent months but have been getting nothing out of it.

'In this round I was getting up and down well and making a few putts, which made all the difference. It has been a great learning year for me and I have learnt a lot of new things about the game. My game is coming along nice and gradually, and maybe by the time I am 24 or 25, I will be contending for some Majors and be in a position to fulfil my ambitions.'

There was that grounded, well-balanced individual speaking again; someone, whom we have already noted, takes ups and downs with the same philosophical approach. This attitude would stand him in good stead – after the lows of the first half of 2008, he would now move on up, just as he had predicted he would do.

A second-round 71 allowed defending champion Brett Rumford back into it – the pair now tied. The Australian carded a second successive round of 67 to reach 8-under-par while Rory managed only a level par 71. But the likes of Alejandro Cañizares, Jean-François Lucquin and Juan Abbate loomed ominously behind them, just a shot back at 7-under-par.

Rory said: 'It's always difficult to follow up a really low round – I've learnt that before. You rarely see a player go 63-64. A 71 was a pretty good effort. It was quite tricky out there and some of the pin positions are quite extreme.'

But he pulled away again on the Saturday, starting with an eagle at the first. 'That eagle settled my nerves,' he told reporters, 'because I was bit nervous going out there. I worked on my ironplay yesterday and obviously it bedded in quite nicely. I don't want to take my foot off the pedal now. I've got a four-shot lead and I want it to be six tomorrow; I'll just try to go out and make birdies. It's a bit like when I was an amateur – I get a few weeks when I'm hitting the ball well and putting well, and you just have to make the most of it.'

But that elusive first pro win was not to be – much to the disappointment also of his manager Chubby Chandler, who had hired a plane to get him from Manchester to Switzerland to celebrate the expected victory. Put simply: Rory blew it, bogeying the 18th to stand level on 271 with Jean-François Lucquin and the Frenchman went on to win the sudden-death playoff. Rory said: 'Obviously I'm disappointed but I can take a lot from this week. I came here after three missed cuts and found a bit of form.'

Indeed, he took his defeat magnanimously, heaping praise on Lucquin and telling him simply: 'You deserved to win.'

In turn, Lucquin was equally pleasant, saying: 'Rory was very good to say what he did. He is a great player, who will win lots in the future – I was not like this at 19.'

In September 2008 Rory also put out a statement on his own blog, www.rorymcilroy.com, to celebrate a year since turning pro: 'If someone had told me a year ago that I'd be in the position I'm in today, I would definitely have taken that. It's been a wonderful first year on the European Tour for me and one I'm sure I'll always remember. I had a great start to my career, making the cut in my first tournament as a professional at the Quinn Insurance British Masters and then going on to finish third at the Alfred Dunhill Links Championship. I secured my Tour card in my third event by finishing joint fourth at The Open de Madrid and it was nice not having to go to Qualifying School and being able to relax a bit and practise for the coming season.

'I've also had a great season so far this year. I'm in the Top 50 on the European Tour Order of Merit and I've achieved all the goals I set for myself, so I'm really pleased with the way things are going.

'I've learnt so much since joining the Tour – I've been to loads of new places and met some lovely new people, and I'm really enjoying experiencing all the different cultures.'

By the end of 2008 he would be even happier as his form continued upwards and he posted four Top 10 finishes in his final six Euro Tour starts of the campaign. A few highlights stand out towards the back end of the year – the Dunhill Links, the Volvo Masters and the Hong Kong Open, in which Rory finished 8th, 39th and 2nd.

Rory admitted he had great hopes of winning at the Dunhill Links – the tournament where he had finished 3rd the previous season. And he was certainly in the running after a strong showing on day two, following his first-round 68 with a 69. He admitted to being lifted by kind words from Padraig Harrington after blowing his chances of winning at the European Masters in Switzerland.

Rory told BBC Sport: 'Padraig called me over on

Wednesday and said, "Hard luck," and that he knew how it felt – we've all blown tournaments that we should have won. He's been second on tour 29 times and learnt how to win; he hasn't had a second place for three years. He told me to keep getting experience, get yourself up there again, and you'll win.

'I need to get into position first to have a chance to do that. If I do, I'm sure my recent experience in Switzerland will help. It didn't quite happen for me then but I'm playing well again this week and I've probably got the easiest course of the three on Saturday. I know the top guys are having to come here to Carnoustie so if I can go out at Kingsbarns and do well, I could be right up there.'

Indeed, he would be right up there – but not at the very top. Sweden's Robert Karlsson beat England's Ross Fisher and Germany's Martin Kaymer in a playoff to clinch the crown, with Rory coming home in 8th place – just 4 off the lead at 6-under-par, he hit 68, 69 and 67 on the 1st, 2nd and 4th rounds. Only a 78 in round three held him back from finishing even higher. At least he had the consolation of finishing above his Irish compatriots. One shot back at 5-under was Padraig Harrington, then came Damien McGrane at 3-under and Graeme McDowell at 2-under.

Rory then exceeded many people's expectations by making it to the Volvo Masters at Valderrama. It was the 21st and final Volvo Masters and was won by Dane Søren Kjeldsen, who claimed the biggest title of his career to date and the €708,330 first prize. The 33-year-old from Aalborg became the first Dane ever to win the Volvo Masters title and the 20th player to have his name on the iconic trophy. 'I'm thrilled, really pleased,' he said afterwards, explaining, 'It was a slightly different kind of challenge from last year when I picked up seven shots over the final round to force myself into a playoff as I had a lead to defend and Martin [Kaymer] started to put a bit of pressure on me.'

Rory said he had enjoyed the experience – and he had done so well to make it to Spain in the first place. As the organisers made clear in a pre-tournament blurb: 'The end-of-season showpiece was only open to the Top 60 players on the European Tour, qualification exclusively for those elite stars within those three-score places based solely on their season-long prize money on the eve of the Volvo Masters.' And Rory had done well enough to make it despite the uneven nature of his first full season as a pro.

By the end of November 2008 he was moving into top gear and getting closer and closer to winning his first pro event. After another great few days' work in the Hong Kong Open, he finished 2nd. On the first day, he hit 70 and followed up with a fine 64 on day two. But he had mixed feelings about his overall display, telling the post-round press conference: 'I feel as though I didn't birdie any of the last five holes and I had wedges into four of them, anyway. A little disappointed but 64 is a great score. I'll have to get off to another good start tomorrow but if I can just get myself into contention on the back nine on Sunday, I feel as if the more I'm there, the more I'll learn and hopefully, I'll be able to close one [a tournament] out sooner or later.

'I played really nicely in Singapore last week and it gives

me a lot of confidence – especially the field that was there last week, beating Phil Mickelson and Adam Scott, and getting myself in the mix. It was sort of self-satisfaction last week but I will try and do a little better this week and get off to a good start in The Race to Dubai.

'The last couple of months have been really good. Ever since Switzerland, I've played really well and it's given me a little boost of confidence and shown me what I can do. I've just got a lot of belief in myself and I feel as if I'm ready to win. And if it's not this week, it might be next week or the week after, but as long as I keep putting myself in these positions, I'll be OK.'

He followed up with a 66 in round three on the Saturday and was happy with his work, saying: 'I did very well today – I was very patient out there, I took my chances when they came on the back nine. The 66 keeps me in and pretty pleased.' He was still firmly in contention – along with surprise package Bernhard Langer, the veteran who was truly enjoying his long weekend in Hong Kong.

Rory paid tribute to his rival, saying: 'He's unbelievable! He's 51 years of age and still out here competing. This golf course is perfect for him – he just positions his ball, left side fairway, right side green, and he just plots himself around here and if he makes a couple of putts, he's going to be well in there. It's good to see him up there.'

But by the Sunday night, neither Rory nor Langer would be celebrating a tournament win. No, that honour was to go to China's Lin Wen-tang, who beat Rory in a playoff – although Rory's 2nd place finish alongside Italian

Francesco Molinari would move the Irishman up to 50th in the world rankings.

Wen-tang walked away with the winner's cheque of $416,660 after becoming the first Asian golfer to win the title in a decade. 'It cannot be described how I feel. All I can do is use my smile to say thank you to you all,' he said.

Rory paid tribute to the winner at the press conference to close the event, but was still disappointed he had lost out – although he accepted that he had learned from the experience and believed he was edging ever closer to his first pro title: 'Lin made two threes on the last, and he probably should have won it in regulation, and then he made two threes in the playoffs. I thought I probably did enough to make three at the first playoff hole and I had an incredible shot for my second shot, but it just wasn't meant to be. But obviously it's still been a great week for me. I'll look back on it, and I've played really well – I couldn't have done much more.

'He had to beat me. I didn't back off and I didn't make any stupid mistakes. It's alright, I'll take all the positives. As long as I can keep putting myself in these positions and feeling the nerves and the adrenaline, I'll know I'm doing things right.

'It puts me in a great position going into the New Year and I have two events left in South Africa. If I don't win there, I'll hopefully win sometime next year. As long as I keep putting myself in these positions, I'll be able to pull through, sooner or later.'

Rory also finished 4th in the Barclays Singapore Open in the November – an Asian Tour result that had him laughing, literally, all the way to the bank. His 4th-place finish and $225,000 prize money meant he had become the youngest golfer to earn €1 million in prize money, even overwhelming Tiger Woods' record. Despite this, he insisted: 'It's not the prize money that's motivating me, it's still a first win and a continued climb up the world rankings. Also, it would be nice to get that Christmas gift of a first invite into next April's US Masters. I'm ranked 80th and a great result in any of my four remaining events this year should get me to the Top 50 and into Augusta.'

He arrived in Singapore having earned €979,000 (£840,000) from 32 European Tour pro career starts and a single appearance earlier that year on the Japan Tour. Rory, 19 at the time, did admit: 'It's nice to reach such a milestone and I'm pinching myself to think I'm not yet 20 and could earn that much money on the golf course but I'm still your normal 19-year-old and it's just that I have matured so much travelling the world, playing golf and being in the company of older players along with meeting sponsors and dignitaries other 19-year-olds would not have access to.'

Of course, he wasn't really your usual 19-year-old. Well, was he? Your regular 19-year-old didn't play professional golf against the world's best players, let alone expect to win against them. But as 2008 edged to a close, Rory McIlroy was on the brink of proving not only had he got what it takes, but he could be a champion, too. Yes, the boy wonder from Northern Ireland was about to go one step further in his already remarkable career – and lift his first-ever professional title.

CHAPTER 8

JUST CHAMPION

Sixteen months after signing with Chubby Chandler, Rory finally ended his quest for that elusive first-title win as a professional. It was an impressive victory at the Dubai Desert Classic and a real statement of intent: he led from start to finish, but had to see off a fine field. The triumph meant that, at 19 years and 273 days, he had become the seventh-youngest winner in European Tour history, the youngest player ever to make it into the world Top 20 rankings and he was now ranked 14th in the world. Rory was also the youngest winner of the Dubai event, beating the previous best of England's David Howell, who had won the 1999 edition when he was 23 and 236 days old.

Indeed, it was a seismic shift in Rory's fortunes – now no

one doubted his ability to win events, let alone his potential. He had come of age.

The boy wonder arrived in Dubai at the end of January 2009 believing that, yes, he was now on the brink of breaking through. As we have noted, the signs were there after he finished 2nd in the Hong Kong Open in November 2008. He had gone on to end the 2008 calendar year at 39th in the world rankings after finishing joint 3rd in the South African Open. This meant he earned the highly prestigious invitation to the US Masters in April 2009.

But it would be that first professional win at the Dubai Desert Classic, on 1 February 2009, that would really make the world of golf sit up and take notice for they now had a new young superstar in their midst. And, in an ironic twist to the tale, it would be Justin Rose whom Rory would beat in a tense final-hole standoff to secure his maiden victory, winning by just one shot – and ironic because many pundits believed, just as Rose had in the early period, that he might just struggle for success after moving from the amateur world to the professional one.

On the Thursday, Rory headed to the green to tee off in determined fashion. He knew it wouldn't be easy but he had faith in his own ability after coming so close to winning in the previous year's European Masters and Hong Kong Open. As the contest developed, he would have to contend with the heat, the humidity and the swirling fog, although this time he never looked like blowing it. On that first day, he shot a brilliant 8-under-par 64 to take the initiative and the lead and was one shot ahead of Robert Karlsson when play was abandoned because of poor visibility. Spain's Gonzalo Fernandez-Castano was a further stroke behind on 66, while South Africa's Charl Schwartzel was also on 6-under, with four holes still to play.

At the press conference after that first day's proceedings, Rory was understandably cock-a-hoop. He was asked if he was playing to win – whether he had reached the stage where he felt confident enough to admit that. To this he replied: 'Yeah, definitely – I want to try and win. I want to try and get into contention every time I go out and play. I've been able to do that quite a lot the last few weeks and I wasn't able to do it last week but hopefully with a good start this week, I'll be able to do it again. As long as I get myself into the position on Sunday, all of those experiences will become valuable. Sooner or later, I'll be able to win one but it's not my main priority. My main priority is just to try to be in contention on the back nine on Sunday. If a win falls my way, then that's fantastic, and if it doesn't, I'll keep trying and keep trying to put myself in the position to win.'

He admitted he had enjoyed playing the round with Mark O'Meara: 'It was great, we had a nice chat on the way around. I used to go over and watch the World Match Play at Wentworth every year and I watched him win in '98, when he beat Tiger. And in '99, Monty beat him in the final, but in the morning he holed a bunker shot out of the trap on 18 and I've got his golf ball from it. He signed it, and I've still got it.'

Rory also said he still sometimes had to pinch himself, such was the joy of playing pro golf with the likes of O'Meara and

Colin Montgomerie while still just 19: 'Ten years is quite a long time in my lifetime but ten years ago, I was rolling the fairways at Wentworth watching O'Meara play. To be able to play with him now, I never thought that – [would be possible]. I always hoped it, but it's just great to be able to play with these guys. For me, it's so cool to be able to walk on the range and say hi to Sergio, just people that I've grown up watching; to be able to get to know them.'

And he was pleased with his day's work on the green: 'I struggled a little last week with my distance control, but I worked on it a little bit this week and I played really nicely out there. It was a great day. I want to get in contention every time I play, and I've been able to do that quite a lot in the last few weeks.'

Double Major champion Mark O'Meara admitted he was impressed by McIlroy's ability – and claimed he was better than Woods at the same age. 'It's his mind and his heart, that's the big element,' O'Meara said. 'Certainly, Rory has those qualities. Ball striking-wise at 19, he's probably better than Tiger [Woods] was at 19. His technique, I think, is better. Certainly, Tiger has developed his game and swing over the years and made modifications to be able to hit the ball pin high but Rory is already doing that and he's 19, so he's already a step ahead.'

They were remarkable words of praise from a great golfer and Rory would declare himself humbled by them. 'It's obviously a huge compliment, probably the highest compliment I could be paid,' he observed. 'Just to be compared to Tiger is mind-blowing. If I can just keep doing what I'm doing, playing well, hopefully a few years down the line I might be able to compete with him.'

Before the second round in Dubai got underway he would also explain how he had started to believe that, yes, he could chalk up that first win because he had come so close to doing it in Switzerland in the Euro Masters the previous year. Rory told reporters: 'I got a lot of confidence [from Switzerland] – it was just one good round. The first round set me off and running, and ever since then I realised how good I could be and how good I hope I can be. That was probably my turning point in my whole year.'

He added that it had also taken time for him to adjust to life on the pro circuit, that it had been 'very difficult' – 'you know, playing golf week-in, week-out, travelling. When you play four weeks in a row, you just want to get home and forget about it for a week or so. But I've learned how to schedule properly and what events to play, and what events not to play and how to plan my season.'

Wise words indeed – the words of a young man with an old head on his shoulders, as some pundits would rightly have it.

Rory was still ahead of the field after shooting a confident 68 on day two, although Henrik Stenson closed the gap to one stroke after hitting a fine 65 to follow his first-round 68 and Justin Rose was also in Rory's slipstream, with a second-round 66 to add to his opening 68.

It would be the Saturday before Rory finished that 68 round after bad light halted play but he then tapped in for an eagle on the third-round 10th to finish the day two shots clear of Australian Richard Green and South Africa's Louis Oosthuizen on 15-under. 'It would be absolutely fantastic to win here,' he told reporters. 'At the moment I am thinking about hitting the 11th tee shot – that's all I can do. We will see what happens tomorrow. I think I've learned a lot from those experiences [last year]. It will stand me in good stead and hopefully if I keep playing the way I am, I'll definitely be able to go close. But avoiding the playoff tomorrow, that's the plan.'

That *was* the plan – and it worked, although it was a close thing. In the end, Rory held his nerve and held on to win his maiden Euro Tour event by one shot after finishing his third round on 67 – and tying up an uneven final round with a 2-under-par 70, giving him a 19-under-par 269 total. That was enough for the one-stroke win over Justin Rose and two over Stenson.

After the triumph, he was on cloud nine. He told reporters at the post-tournament press conference that he was 'delighted' and explained how he had won: 'I got myself into a great position, middle of the back nine, and then let a few shots slip and Justin birdied a couple as well, so I fought back. It was nice to just hold it together on the last and get a great up-and-down for the victory. I went to the 18th tee knowing that I still had a one-shot lead, so I knew that Justin needed to birdie it.

'After the tee shot, I never thought that I was going to make bogey. I hit a perfect lay-up shot and he just hit his through the fairway. I hit my third shot about seven yards too far and left myself with a pretty tricky up-and-down. I managed to

Above left: Sixteen-year-old Rory McIlroy tees off at the 2005 Irish Open. That year, he became the youngest ever winner of both the West of Ireland Championship and the Irish Close Championship.

Above right: Rory at the 2007 Open de Portugal.

Below: Playing in his first Open Championship at Carnoustie in 2007, Rory won the silver medal for the highest-placed amateur.

Above left: Rory in a spot of bother at the 2007 Alfred Dunhill Links Championship.

Above right: At the Mastercard Masters in Australia in November 2007.

Below: Rory in action at the Omega European Masters in 2008, held in the beautiful Swiss mountains.

Above: Sharing a joke with football legend Sir Bobby Charlton after the second round of the 2008 Alfred Dunhill Links Championship.

Below: Rory celebrates winning the Dubai Desert Classic in February 2009.

Above left: Rory lines up a shot during the 2009 Irish Open in Baltray, County Louth.

Above right: Rory with his caddy, JP Fitzgerald, during the PGA Championship at Wentworth in 2009.

Below: Success on the golf course has led to Rory gaining huge popularity among fans.

Above: Northern Ireland is emerging as a breeding ground for top golfers – here, Rory is pictured with fellow Northern Irish stars Graeme McDowell and Darren Clarke.

Below: Rory celebrates with Great Britain and Ireland captain Paul McGinley after winning the inaugural Vivendi Trophy With Severiano Ballesteros in 2009. The competition pits the best players in Europe against Britain and Ireland's elite golfers.

Above: Rory and his father, Gerry, at Carnoustie in 2009.

Below: As one of golf's biggest rising stars, Rory is always in demand with the world's media.

Above left: Rory prepares to chip the ball from the water's edge during the third round of the 2009 Dubai World Championship.

Above right: Rory kicks off 2010 with an appearance at the Abu Dhabi Golf Championship, where he finished third.

Below: Another trophy for Rory – and his first PGA Tour win, at the 2010 Quail Hollow Championship.

Above left: Rory heads to the 18th fairway at the 2010 British Open at St Andrews.

Above right: Saluting the fans at the end of the fourth round.

Below: Talking tactics with caddy JP Fitzgerald at the US PGA Championship in August 2010.

take a few deep breaths and compose myself. It was probably one of the best bunker shots I've ever played. To knock the putt in as well was absolutely great.'

He admitted the victory was 'a monkey off my back' and said he was now motivated to win another tournament as soon as possible: 'I go out with the same mindset every week and try to get myself into contention going into the back nine on Sunday – that's my goal every week. If I'm able to do that, it's great. And I was able to do it here. I said at the start of the week that as long as I put myself in these positions, sooner or later, I'll be able to close one out. Fortunately for me, I was able to do that this week. I've moved up a step and I want to try and keep getting better and better.

'Your success only makes you more motivated to try to do better. I've realised that I've become a very good player and I just want to keep trying to practise harder and improve. It's definitely a monkey off my back. If I had not won today, having a six-shot lead, it would have been pretty tough to take and it would have been hard to come back from that, but I was able to scrape in at the end.'

He was asked what he had learned – and if he could put any learning experiences to good use. 'Golf is such a funny game – you can be so far ahead, but the guys can still pay you back and that's what happened,' he said. 'Justin made a great eagle on 13, great birdie on 17, and my lead was down to one and you sort of have to reassess. But all of these situations and all of these positions that I've put myself in, it's all experience and I'm gathering it, week-by-week. Obviously the experiences that I've had in the past helped me today and hopefully today's will help me in the future.'

Yet again, wise words from a young man.

Rory was also keen to pay tribute to his mum Rosie and dad Gerry, declaring: 'This win is definitely for my parents, who were here. They have never been pushy, they have done so much for me and it's nice to be able to repay them in some way.'

As his fame continued to spread across the globe, back in Ireland he was being hailed a sporting hero. Irish Sports Minister Martin Cullen led the tributes, saying, 'I am delighted that Rory McIlroy has won the Dubai Desert Classic, his first victory on the European Tour. In terms of his golf career, this is a prestigious win for such a young player and his thrilling victory, which comes after a run of resolute play at this important tournament, underlines Rory McIlroy's position as one of the leading up-and-coming players in world golf. I know that this victory will be a prelude to many more famous victories to come for this promising golfer.'

And he was right about that. The fans also wanted to pat Rory on the back after his momentous moment. One lifelong fan, Rob, said: 'This "kid" does seem to be the real deal. I think he lost a couple of playoffs recently after he sort of "stumbled in" to end up in them to begin with. I thought those might affect his psyche a little – wrong!' And another fan, Richie, said: 'I like Rory's game a lot. Good-looking golf swing, and was glad to see him come away with a victory at Dubai.' Another Rory supporter added: 'McIlroy's victory at

Dubai was impressive considering the very fine field that he had to beat and leading from wire to wire was superb considering the "kid" is only 19. I think it is a bit of a disservice to start the Tiger comparisons just yet, wait a few years. He does have a good game and it doesn't seem lacking in any area. He is learning, and learning fast, and I'm sure will be a force for all the pros to contend with.'

And so Rory had done it – got the monkey off his back with that first win. Now he intended to prove it wasn't a one-off; that he did indeed have what it takes to give Tiger & Co. a run for their money on a regular basis.

CHAPTER 9

THE HEAT
IS ON

Rory's fine form from Dubai continued in 2009 – just weeks after lifting his first Euro Tour trophy in Dubai, he proved his mettle in the Accenture World Matchplay Championships in reaching the quarter-finals. It was another important notch on his belt as he showed the pro golfing world that he was here to stay – and here to become the best.

In the first round of the event he defeated Louis Oosthuizen 2 & 1, in the second he beat Hunter Mahan 1-up – and in the third ended the hopes of Tim Clark 4 & 3. He only bowed out when he came across the eventual winner Geoff Ogilvy in the quarter-finals, 2 & 1.

Naturally, he was disappointed to have exited in the quarters but maintained he had done all he could. He said he had enjoyed the experience and would learn from it – and also predicted, correctly, that Ogilvy would go on to lift the coveted trophy. Rory said: 'I couldn't have done much more. Geoff just played great today – I expected it as he is a Major champion and has won two world golf championships. I made a few birdies, but Geoff made a few more and I couldn't do anything about it. I think he will be very hard to beat.'

At the post-event press conference he was asked if he changed tactics when up against someone like Ogilvy, who was making so many birdies. He answered: 'A little. He got two up on me after 12 and didn't birdie the par five so I managed to get one back at me, but then he threw three in a row at me to finish me off. I just tried to keep doing what I was doing and making birdies, and it was very nice to make that putt on the 16th to keep the match going, but then he holed one on 17 to shut me out. But I have taken a lot from it. It is my first time in America and I have played great, which has given me a lot of confidence. I have hit it great and battled well when I needed to – it's been great.'

So, how did he rate his final morning's work in the Championship?

'I played pretty well. I made a couple of bogeys, but some birdies and didn't do too many things wrong and I just came up against Geoff, who was playing great. He threw eight birdies at me and I just couldn't keep it going. It was nice to hole the putt on 16 to keep the match alive, but when he threw three in a row I couldn't do anything about it. I've learnt that I can compete out there and I am able to hang with the best in the world. It is great for my confidence that I have come out in my first event in America and done so well.'

It was pointed out to him that Tiger Woods had not won 'a tournament like you did in the desert.' He was then asked if he now craved Woods' No. 1 spot, if this was his ultimate ambition. 'It would be great to get that accolade one day,' he admitted, 'but I am just trying to play my golf, keep improving and see where it gets me. I am not trying to set any major goals like that as Tiger is Tiger. He has been the best in the world for the last 10 years and I see no reason why he won't be for another few years – I just want to try and get in the Top 10 in the world and see how it goes from there.'

He continued to play on the PGA Tour until May 2009 and finished tied for 13th at the Honda Classic, tied for 20th at the WGC-CA Championship and tied for 19th at the Shell Houston Open. At the latter, he said that he wanted eventually to join the PGA TOUR but was adamant that for the next few years he expected to play primarily on the European Tour.

One of his own personal highlights of 2009 came in April when he appeared at The Masters in his first Major tournament as a professional. He did himself credit, finishing tied for 20th place, 2 shots-under-par for the event. Of the players to make the cut, McIlroy achieved the third-highest average driving distance, beaten only by Dustin Johnson and Andres Romero.

Before action got underway at The Masters, Rory had sounded like an excited schoolboy. He said: 'I'm very excited to be here. It's my second trip to Augusta, but first Masters week. It's great. It's a huge thrill to be here, and it's been a dream of mine for a long time to be able to play in The Masters. For that dream to finally come true is a pretty special feeling.

'It's a week that I'm going to enjoy and hopefully, I'll be playing pretty well. Hopefully, I can pick up some valuable experience. If it doesn't quite work out this week, I'll hopefully have plenty more times to try to do well.'

He revealed that he was also enjoying his new star status, especially after fans queued to get his autograph: 'It's great. Obviously I've received a lot of attention the last few weeks and you know you're doing things well when you are. I wasn't able to sign that many autographs – I was rushing to the range to hit a few balls before I went out. After I've done this [press conference], I'll sign as many as I can.'

Asked if he ever worried that he might be being pushed in at the deep end too early, too quickly and suffer – as, say, Justin Rose seemed to – he responded: 'I think it's down to the mental capacity that a certain individual has. I'm not one to get overwhelmed by much; I just go about my business and play my golf and if it's good enough then so be it. But playing on Tour at such an early age, I don't feel like a 19-year-old – I feel I've matured very quickly since coming on Tour. It's obviously a great position to be in, and one that I've wanted to get to for a long time. Now that I'm here, I want to make the most of it and become the best player that I can.'

He said he wasn't nervous and wasn't overawed; that the win in Dubai had done the world of good for his confidence and self-esteem: 'It gave me a lot of confidence, beating a field like that, that had at the time the No. 2 player in the world – that had maybe seven or eight of the Top 15 in the world. It gave me a lot of motivation to try and go on and do better. To get into the Majors and to get into the big championships, it's just another step in the progression and hopefully I can keep progressing for a long time.'

After The Masters Rory played in two more events on the PGA Tour, including his first appearance at The Players Championship, where he was cut. He then returned to Europe and finished 5th at the BMW PGA Championship and 12th at the European Open.

At the BMW he was asked if he ever pinched himself at the way his career was soaring upwards and how he kept his feet on the ground, how he coped with ever-growing stardom when he was just 20. He said: 'It's still very early in my career and to achieve what I have has been very good, but I've worked hard for it and I was given the talent by someone and I've made the most of it. I've tried to become the best golfer that I can. I'm going to try and keep working hard, and try to get better.

'When I get home, most of my friends are at university so they are either back in Belfast or there's a few in Dundee, a few in Edinburgh, a few in Newcastle. But every chance that I get to see them and see my family when I'm home, I do, and that's why I feel it's so important to take breaks and to take a couple of weeks off here or there – to go home and relax and get away from all this.

'Like I said before, it's like two different lives – I've got my life out here where I'm working hard and trying to win golf tournaments, and my life back home where I've got my family and my friends, my girlfriend and just trying to be a normal guy.'

And the top-five finish in the BMW had added to his ever-growing confidence: 'This is a great week for me because it's put me back on track, another top-five finish. I feel as if I've got the game to go and win there next week [at the European Open], so this is hopefully a good building block for the rest of the season.'

Of course, he would not win at the European but it was good to see how he was progressing as a golfer and a person, how he was starting to believe in himself and flourishing as a result. That newfound confidence would surface during the rest of 2009, in particular as he chalked up two tremendous results in two of the next three Majors in which he would participate.

At the US Open in June, the American media were keen to build up the idea that Rory would now be the main contender to their hero, Tiger. But he played it down, adding he was not going to obsess about beating Woods: 'If he plays the way he did the last round at Memorial, then no [he wouldn't beat him]. But I can't control what he does or what anyone else does in the field, I just have to go out and play my golf. If it's good enough, it's good enough. If it's not, then so be it.

'So, guys don't go into Majors thinking I have to do this to beat Tiger, I have to do that to beat Tiger – they go in and they concentrate on their own game. If their own game at the end of the day isn't good enough then that's the way it goes.'

Rory finished tied for 10th in his first US Open at Bethpage and declared himself 'delighted' to be on equal billing with the likes of Sergio Garcia and 2003 Masters winner Mike Weir. In the final round he carded a 2-under-par 68 to achieve his first Top 10 finish in a Major.

He said: 'It's been a great week – a long one – but I feel like I have done very well. I have made a great start to my Majors career: 10th here and 20th in The Masters. I feel I have the game to compete in Majors and those results have given me a lot of confidence. I knew I shot a couple of 70s and 72s in the first rounds and I knew the guys were lighting it up a bit. I knew if I just hung around and stayed patient, around level par would be a very good result in this tournament and that's what I was trying to do today to get back to level. It didn't quite happen – I got it to plus 1 for the tournament but finished at plus 2. But I can take a lot from the week.'

Rory then went on to play in his first Open as a pro, but it was not as successful as he might have hoped. He turned up at Turnberry in Scotland as one of the favourites and said he felt he could do justice to that tag. 'I've proved to myself that I do have the game to get around Major championships,' he declared. 'It's about staying patient – as long as I stay patient and don't get ahead of myself, I know my game can stand up

to the hardest test in golf. I sometimes say to myself this is only
your second Open championship, you'll have 20 or 30 more
of these — there's no point trying to rush into things. But
there's also a part of me that says, "You know you've got the
game to do well here."

'It's a balance between having the right expectations and
trying to fulfil those. It's hard because walking up the 18th,
you catch yourself thinking, "Oh, what if this happens or
that happens, how good would it be to win The Open." It's
something you've got to deal with — I'm getting better and
better at it every week. I've got a little bit of form. I had a
good session on the range last night with Michael Bannon,
my coach, and I feel like I'm hitting the ball really well going
into the tournament. I just hope to go out there and keep it
out of the rough. If I can shoot somewhere around 70 every
day, I think that will be pretty good.'

He also felt the fact that Turnberry was a links course
would tell in his favour: 'The greens remind me quite a bit
of Carnoustie, the way there's a few runoffs and the way the
bunkers sort of set up at you. And obviously I've played a lot
of links golf growing up — I hope it should help me. I feel as
if I've got all the shots that are required to play good golf on
links courses. We don't get to play a lot on the Tour — it's nice
to get back to a links course. It's like riding a bicycle: once
you're on it, you somehow remember all the shots you need
for it, little pitch-and-runs and little punch shots into the
wind and so forth. I feel very comfortable on links; hopefully
that will show this week.'

The dream wasn't to be — Rory ended up tied for 47th,

with Stewart Cink beating Tom Watson in a playoff to win the 138th Open and complete his maiden Major victory. But Rory is a young man who never gives up, who learns from adversity and determines to use that experience to move forward once again. Which is just what he did after the setback at Turnberry, finishing tied for 3rd in the US PGA Championship in Minnesota with a 3-under-par total of 285 (with rounds of 71, 73, 71 and 70). It was his best performance yet in a Major – and one that boosted his confidence after the setback at Turnberry.

Even before the first round, he had felt he was going to have a good tournament when asked by reporters how he thought he had fared so far in Majors. He said: 'For my first year in the Majors, I've done very well. I've had a Top 20 at The Masters, finished 10th at the US Open, but was pretty disappointed at Turnberry not to finish higher. The thing about Majors is it's almost easier to get yourself into position to do well rather than in a normal tournament because you don't have to make as many birdies. You can just grind a few pars out and shoot a few decent scores around level par and you'll know that you'll not be far away.

'I've learned how to be patient in these events because you have to be. You can't go out chasing scores in these tournaments because a couple of bad shots here and there can cost you two or three shots, and two or three shots in these tournaments is a lot. It's about trying to put yourself into position to where, going into the last day, you can have a chance to contend and put in a good finish.'

On his final round Rory started with a double bogey but

notched four birdies on the front nine to make the turn on
2-under-par. A bogey on 12 was redeemed by a birdie on 14
and four pars on the way home brought Rory that tied 3rd
place, with old pal Lee Westwood.

Afterwards, Rory was understandably jubilant. He
explained how he had kept his nerve despite that double-
bogey start: 'The first hole has not been kind to me this week
– I've had three bogeys and I didn't get off to the best start.
But after that I just played really good golf. I missed a couple
of chances on the way in, but I got a couple of really good
up-and-downs on 17 and 18, which got me where I was. For
the last Major of the year, I feel as if I've put in a really strong
finish and I'm really pleased with myself.

'I've been very patient – I didn't get flustered when I made
a 6 at the first, I knew that I had a few chances on the front
nine to get it back. I had four birdies after that on the front
nine to turn at 2-under and the back nine was playing very
tough today. To shoot level par on that back nine with this
wind, I felt was a really good effort. I just stayed patient and
I knew I would have chances out there. I felt a 70 out there
[with crosswinds affecting play] was very good.'

The reporters also pointed out 17 birdies in a Major on a
course that proved difficult to play was also truly impressive.
Rory agreed: 'Yes, it is, considering I only made five birdies
last week at Akron, so it's been a bit of a difference. But I like
the greens out here and I felt as if I could do well on this
golf course. It's a big, long golf course which usually suits me
and I felt comfortable on it since the day we arrived.

'It's been a great week for me. I'm now looking forward

to getting home and will reflect on my play in the Majors during the couple weeks I have off – I feel very pleased the way I played them, I have a lot to build on. I have a lot of momentum going into the Majors next year. This is only my first year in the Majors, so I learned a few things on my way. Hopefully they will help me next year to get in a couple of better finishes than just the Top 10 or Top 5.'

The brilliant result and joy on Rory's face contrasted sharply with Tiger Woods' depression as he unbelievably blew what had seemed an inevitable victory, allowing South Korea's Y. E. Yang to sneak home. The PGA's own website (PGA.com) best summed up the shock outcome: 'On Sunday, with the world watching and expecting Tiger Woods to march confidently to his 15th major championship win, a far different story unfolded. Yang, a 37-year-old, second-year player on the PGA Tour, entered the final round of the 91st PGA Championship at Hazeltine tied for second with Padraig Harrington, trailing Woods by two shots. It seemed like Yang was simply going to have a front-row seat to witness Woods do what he does best – close out another Major.

'Until Sunday, Woods was a perfect 14-of-14 when leading a Major after 54 holes. But as rays of sunshine poked abundantly through scattered clouds over the 18th hole Sunday evening, the formerly insurmountable Woods was finally undone. From 210 yards away in the left side of the fairway and with an obstructed view to the green because of a cluster of towering trees, Yang delivered a glorious 3-hybrid approach shot that landed like a feather and settled just six feet from the hole, setting up a fist pump-inducing birdie to put an exclamation point on an unexplainable, unbelievable triumph over the world's No. 1 player. Yang's final tally was 8-under-par 280, a shocking three shots better than Woods, the second-place finisher.'

And the outcome gave Rory a further lift after his third place finish: he finally knew for sure that the previously invincible Tiger was now very beatable. The era of the Northern Irishman at the expense of the legend was getting closer and closer, no doubt about it. As one man moved ever upward, another seemed on an inexorable downward spiral. The times they were a changin' in the golfing echelons.

At the end of September 2009, Rory chalked up more success in helping Great Britain and Ireland win the Vivendi Trophy for the fifth successive time. In his first team event as a pro, he beat world No. 5 Henrik Stenson on the final green in Paris. Graeme McDowell followed up with a 3&2 victory over Robert Karlsson – which meant Continental Europe had lost with seven games still on the course. The Brits eventually ran out 16½–11½ winners.

Rory went round in a 6-under-par 65 and said he hoped the display would earn him a Ryder Cup place a year on: 'I'd be lying if I said my hands weren't a little shaky over the putt on the last. It's great for the team as well because we haven't really got off to the best of starts today and it's good to put a point on the board early. It's been a fantastic week and I'll be very disappointed if I don't make the Ryder Cup now.

'This is my first professional team event and I've played very, very well. It's been a very good week. To beat Henrik in the singles is a nice feeling – he's played a couple of Ryder Cups and he's in the Top 5 in the world.'

As 2009 drew to a close, things would get even better for Rory. He finished the season in 2nd place behind Lee Westwood in the inaugural European Tour Race to Dubai. Then, in the November, he entered the Top 10 of the world rankings for the first time – the youngest player to do so since Sergio Garcia. The year concluded with Rory ranked 9th in the world and with the legendary Gary Player praising the Northern Irish boy as the 'most exciting young player in the world.'

Lavish praise indeed, but as 2010 dawned Rory would prove that he was worthy of it. Within four months, he would have won his first PGA tournament to add to the Dubai Euro Tour event already under his belt. The world was literally at his feet, although he would first have to suffer a minor blip.

CHAPTER 10

BACK UP AGAINST THE WALL

It was to be a mixed build-up to that first win on the PGA circuit: Rory started well enough in the Abu Dhabi Golf Championship and the Dubai Desert Classic but then tailed off with a string of disappointing results and a spell away from events due to a bad back. But as he headed off for Abu Dhabi in the United Arab Emirates, leaving the cold and misery of a UK winter behind for the warmth and sunshine of the Middle East, he was on a high. He had told his father Gerry that this could be his year – he was feeling confident and knew that he was shaping up to play the best golf of his career. Even a bout of swine flu, which had certainly laid him low, failed to douse his high spirits: he knew he was getting better and better, and that with each experience, whether good or bad, he was learning and mastering the art of the game as well as himself and his own fears and deficiencies.

He was a work in progress, albeit a work not far off becoming a masterpiece as the Quail Hollow victory would confirm in April. First, he had a double mission in the Middle East – in Abu Dhabi and Dubai – and he would complete both satisfactorily.

When Rory and his entourage arrived in Abu Dhabi, he spent some time looking around the city and relaxing before heading off for his first press conference of the New Year. Summing up just how successful 2009 had been, he said: 'Yeah, it was a great year for me all round – getting my first win early on in the season in Dubai and then kicking on from there and putting in a lot of really solid performances. I had a great chance going into the Dubai World Championship to take the first Race to Dubai title but there was another guy that was just a little too good that week. But it was a great season and it was a long season as well. It was nice to get home and have a bit of a break over the Christmas period but lovely to be back out in the sunshine here and practising again and getting ready for the 2010 season.'

He also admitted that the pressure was now greater but said he felt confident enough to handle it. 'There probably will be more pressure,' he conceded. 'I got myself into the Top 10 in the world, which brings a few pressures in itself, trying to stay there and trying to move higher. It's a lot more difficult to move from 10th to 5th than it is from 40th to 20th, so I've still got to keep playing well. One of my big goals this year is to win more events. I felt as if I put myself in a lot of good positions last year to win and to be able to only win once was slightly disappointing, so I would like to capitalise on the good positions that I put myself in.'

By the end of play on the Saturday he was right in contention for the Abu Dhabi title behind Germany's Martin Kaymer, who shot his third straight 5-under 67 to take a one-stroke lead. Kaymer would be tough to beat, Rory knew that – after all, he had won the tournament in 2008 and tied for 2nd in 2009.

Rory and Ian Poulter had both shot 67 on the Saturday and were tied for 2nd behind Kaymer. But Kaymer was playing in some pain and there were doubts as to whether he would last the distance – he had had a plate inserted in his foot after an accident the previous summer. Kaymer admitted he was faced with a regular dilemma with the injury: 'If I have the plate taken out, I will need another two to two-and-a-half weeks to recover and I never really get a break for three weeks during the season. I don't want to miss tournaments in a Ryder Cup year but I do seem to be able to play good golf with it still in place. There are certain shots where I still have to be careful when I play with the ball below my feet; it hurts a bit. But I do like this course – I always seem to play well here because all the tee shots seem to suit my eye.'

Rory also enjoyed playing the course and he felt he could pounce if Kaymer should start to struggle on the final day. After Saturday's round, he told reporters: 'Today was great. I thought the scoring was very good considering the conditions. You know, it was quite windy out there – it was getting quite gusty towards the end. I'm really pleased with 67 out there. I didn't make too many mistakes and put myself in a great position going into tomorrow. It should be a good battle tomorrow – we are all playing very well, so it should be an interesting day.'

It was certainly that – and a relatively successful one, too. OK, Rory wouldn't scoop the crown but he would show that he was still up there with the best and progressing. That progress was highlighted by a 3rd placed finish, an improvement on the tied 5th of the previous year – scores of 66, 69, 67 and 67 helped him to up his game in the UAE. And there was certainly no disgrace in finishing runner-up to a talent like Kaymer, whose win now propelled him above Tiger Woods as the World No. 2.

A top-seven finish would have pushed Kaymer beyond Tiger, but Kaymer closed with a 66 for a tournament-record 24-under-par total of 268. 'He's killing us,' admitted Retief Goosen. 'I have never seen anything above 20-under round here.'

And Padraig Harrington joined in the praise, adding: 'He's probably the most formidable player in the world when he is leading. He seems to intimidate the rest of the field into believing that if he gets in front, he is going to win.'

After his win Kaymer exhibited a modesty that Rory would tell friends he was 'very impressed by.' The German said: 'It's just the perfect course for me. It was more difficult, but I hit a lot of fairways and my putting was amazing. It was just one of those weeks when everything goes my way. I never expected my career to go this fast. There was not a lot to improve this week, but there's always something and I'll be working on my game before Qatar in two weeks.'

Rory also paid his compliments to Kaymer, saying: 'We played great golf, which is one of the most important things. We made birdies and hung in there. Martin made a great birdie at the last, set up by a great tee shot. It's incredible the way he has come back from having the plate in his foot. This is his fifth win, and he's a great player. I'm sure I'll have a lot of battles with him over not just this year but in future years, and he'll be a great addition to the Ryder Cup team.'

He added that he was also pleased with his own efforts that weekend; they had resulted in him moving up from 12th to 7th in the world rankings. Having produced three eagles and 18 birdies, he said: 'Martin and Ian played very, very well today and I didn't get off to the best of starts, but I kept patient and hung in there and made a couple nice birdies towards the end. It just wasn't enough but it's still a great way to start the season, last group and going down the last one behind and getting juices flowing again. It was a nice feeling and hopefully that will set the tone for the rest of the year.'

It would certainly set the tone for the next tournament, also in the sunny, humid Middle East – the Dubai Desert Classic. The year before, of course, Rory had become the event's youngest winner at 19 years and 273 days, beating the previous best of England's David Howell, who had won the 1999 when he was 23 and 236 days old. This time around, Rory was one of six tied for first place after the opening day

– starting his title defence with a 4-under-par 68 to finish alongside Alexander Norén, Charl Schwartzel, Jeev Milkha Singh, Edoardo Molinari and Stephen Dodd.

Rory was happy with his start – especially as he had been forced to contend with wind and sand. He said: 'It was very tricky out there. It was windy and sandy and dusty, and I did get off to a rough start but I made a very lucky birdie on the third and that got me back to level par after three. I knew the front nine was playing a lot tougher than the back nine so I knew if I kept it around level par the front nine, I was doing OK. Then if I could take advantage of the par 5s on the back nine, which I was able to do. I birdied a couple of them and overall it was a great day's work, so I'm in good spirits going into tomorrow morning.'

By the end of round two, however, he had slipped to tied 5th after shooting a 70, leaving him with a 6-under-par total of 138, but he was still hopeful he could put together another two top rounds to retain his crown. He said: 'It was a solid day and the conditions are still pretty tricky out there. Six-under-par going into the weekend is not too bad and only one shot behind at the minute – I still feel pretty good.' A double bogey at the last hole had proved costly for him, with Thongchai Jaidee of Thailand now taking the lead after shooting a six-under-par. The former Thai army paratrooper made six birdies to record a 66 and finish the day 8-under.

He would retain the lead – but in a four-way tie with Miguel Angel Jiménez, Alvaro Quiros and Lee Westwood – with a third-round 69 and a 205 total. Rory's third-round 69 meant he was still tied 5th, now on a total of 207. Afterwards he admitted to being 'frustrated' with his day: 'It was a day of frustration with everything; it was just a really slow start of day – I couldn't really get anything going, I couldn't get any momentum out there. I didn't really hit it, the par 5s weren't the best today so obviously you need to take advantage of them out here, which I didn't. But I'm still within a couple of shots of the lead, I'm still in with a great chance. I was flat the whole day, ever since the first tee shot, just a little flat – I just struggled to really get anything going.'

On the final round he could only manage a 73, which left him tied for 6th on a 280 8-under-par total. He had relinquished his title – and that was disappointing. The new holder was Miguel Angel Jiménez, who came home in an 11-under-par 277.

Rory was never really in with a shout after bogeys at the 7th and 9th left him with too much work to do down the back nine and at the press conference afterwards, he sounded choked up, saying: 'I'm obviously very disappointed at the minute. I didn't play very well today, and didn't take my chances and just was a bit of a struggle, really. It doesn't matter anymore – I want to win and didn't even put myself in a position today to do that. I didn't really get anything going.

'I suppose it was very difficult out there today with the wind but I played OK the first few holes and I just didn't take my chances. Like 20-foot putts, you know, you need to hole maybe two or three out of ten and I just didn't hole. I'm disappointed with not putting any pressure on the guys. It was hard to get momentum, and I should have made birdie on three and I hit a good putt on four that didn't go in for birdie. I just wasn't able to get birdies early – and I needed to do.'

Small consolation that his pal Lee Westwood also blew up: Westwood had the chance of beating Spaniard Jiménez in a playoff, but lost out.

By the time of the WGC–Accenture Match Play Championship in mid-February, Rory was starting to suffer from a sore back. His agent Chubby Chandler revealed that his client had stretched ligaments in his lower back, adding this would not stop him from heading to Arizona for the Match Play Championship.

Chandler explained that the injury had resulted from 10 days of practice in January 2010 to prepare for the new season and then playing two tournaments in three weeks. He added that Rory would rest and have massage therapy before the tournament – and hopefully this would solve the problem. Fourth seed Rory certainly did not seem to be struggling in his opening match – indeed he played some wonderful, battling golf. He was four down to American Kevin Na early on and still two behind with only four holes left, but eagled the next and won on the final green. The display was all the more impressive – and important – as he put it on in front of Colin Montgomerie, who would be Ryder Cup skipper in the following October and had already said he had great hopes for Rory in the event at Celtic Manor.

Before the tournament teed off, Rory was asked how his life had changed in the year since he had last been to Tucson.

He said: 'I've gotten two new dogs. I'd like to think that I haven't changed at all but I've taken up my PGA Tour membership, which has been a big change. Apart from that it's just been great to be playing golf and to be playing good golf – and I just want to try to keep it going. I'll probably not think about it too much because if I sit back and think, that's probably when I'll start to not play my best.'

But was he worried that a sore back might wreck his chances? He told the press conference: 'No, it's fine. I rested last week. I hit balls on Friday for an hour and a half and it was fine. In the actual action of hitting the golf swing it's fine but a couple of hours after I hit the balls on Friday, I felt it a little bit. And then today I played 18 holes and I hit great golf shots so in the motion of swinging a golf club, it's fine. But I have to think about the way I pick up the ball out of the hole and tee it up. But it's not painful, it's just like a niggle.'

He also revealed for the first time that he was contemplating hiring a mental coach to toughen him up still further: 'I've talked to Chubby [Chandler] about it and it couldn't hurt. Most guys go to see mental coaches when they're playing poorly, but I want to be able to turn these Top 5s and Top 3s into wins and I think that getting someone on the mental side of things might be able to help me get to that stage.'

After beating Kevin Na one up in the first round, Rory was happy with the victory but admitted he had not particularly enjoyed it. He explained: 'I definitely didn't make it very easy for myself today. I got off to a very slow start and Kevin got off to a very good start – 4 down through 6 – so it wasn't looking too good. I just hung in there and played some good golf around the turn. I hit a really good drive on 15 and then to go square through 16, I knew I was in a pretty good position. I hung in well and had a great drive on the last, which put him under a little bit of pressure and he hit a bit of a wayward one. I was pretty fortunate to get through today. I'll need to play a lot better if I want to progress into the latter stages of the tournament.'

But he didn't improve – a fact confirmed by his loss to Oliver Wilson in the second round on a play-off hole. As usual when things hadn't quite gone to plan, Rory was honest enough to stand up and be counted. He said: 'I didn't play great but you don't have to play well in match play to get through – you just have to beat your opponent. And I wasn't quite able to do that today. Ollie played well when he needed to and I had a couple of chances to take control of the match and I didn't, and that was really the key.

'But it's match play, it's very fickle. I could have played a lot better and lost. I could have played a little worse and won. It's just the way it is. But now I'm just looking forward to going to Florida and playing in the Honda.'

However, the Florida trip would not prove therapeutic as Rory finished tied for 40th – a considerable disappointment when you consider the previous year, as a 19-year-old, he had tied for 13th. Some critics were starting to question his progress and wondering whether he would ever shake off the back problem that was clearly restricting him. But they needn't have worried: two months after the flop in Florida, Rory was all smiles as he picked up his first PGA trophy. Yes, he was truly back in business.

CHAPTER 11

NOT SO HOLLOW

It was the weekend he truly came of age as a pro golfer of the highest level; the weekend when he set record after record and proved not only had he put his minor blip behind him, he should now be accepted and regarded as one of the real contenders of modern era golf. No wonder he was smiling, hugging and shaking hands with all comers after the win at the Quail Hollow Championship in Charlotte, North Carolina – his first triumph on the PGA Tour and the second of his burgeoning career – and all at the tender age of 20.

The Associated Press best summed up this remarkable achievement when they said: 'All the buzz about Rory McIlroy came to life Sunday at the Quail Hollow Championship with one dazzling shot after another in a record round that made him the PGA Tour's youngest winner since Tiger Woods.

'Explosive as ever, the 20-year-old from Northern Ireland was 5-under over the final five holes to set the course record at 10-under 62 and win by four shots over Masters champion Phil Mickelson. McIlroy finished in style, rolling in a 40-foot birdie putt on the 18th hole and thrusting his fist into the air.'

And who could blame him for such a public show of joy? The boy had earned it – and all the accolades coming his way. He had overwhelmed a class field, including Woods and Mickelson. Indeed, *World Golf* wondered if this was the end of an era with Rory replacing Tiger as the figurehead – 'A simple coincidence or the start of a new era? That's the debate after 20-year-old Rory McIlroy dominated the weekend at the Quail Hollow Championship in Charlotte while Tiger Woods went home after missing the cut – badly. McIlroy also stormed past another relative "old guard" player: Phil Mickelson, who's final round 68 wasn't nearly enough to chase down the Northern Irishman.'

Rory admitted he had been laid low after a series of poor results – which also included missing the cut at The Masters in April 2010. He told BBC Sport that his Masters showing had been 'pretty frustrating' after he finished 7-over at Augusta: 'I felt as if I played OK, but didn't get much out of the week. There were some positives to take from it as I did hit the ball a lot better than I had been doing for the last few weeks and I just need to sharpen up around the greens and get my scoring back to where it was at the end of last year.

I know I have the game to contend at tournaments and it is just a matter of going out there and shooting the scores. I haven't been doing that and I'll just have to go back to the drawing board.'

But he had ruled out the break that he had been talking about after his Masters' misery, saying: 'I was just off the golf course when I made those remarks and I maybe just over-reacted a bit – I wasn't really thinking straight, having just missed the cut in a Major for the first time. I have played six Majors and that was the first cut I have missed, but I have got a couple of weeks off now before I go back to the States. I will put in some good work in the next couple of weeks and should be in the right frame of mind to go to America and improve on my performances.' Just as well he didn't take that enforced break – otherwise he might well have missed out on a groundbreaking maiden PGA victory at Quail Hollow!

Rory arrived at Charlotte with the thermometer touching 24°C/75°F, which pleased him as he had always made it clear he preferred playing in the warmth rather than drizzle, rain and cold. The heat would certainly be on for the boy wonder as he struggled through rounds one and two, though.

After the first round he was 1-under-par with a 72 and just made the cut on the number after a second-round 73. But his weekend really took off on the Saturday – and as for the Sunday – well, that was just a truly amazing round of golf as he blistered the course and shocked both press and public. He had come back from the dead to win the title.

On the Saturday he seemed a different player, blowing off the cobwebs that had seen him struggle on the Thursday and

Friday, and turning in a round to enforce the message that he truly meant business. It was as if he was blasting away the frustrations and agonies of the last couple of months – and the failure to even make the cut in his previous tournament, The Masters – as he raced to a scorching 6-under-par 66, which left him 5-under-par and well in line for glory on the final day. His brilliant round included nine birdies and he was beaming at the press conference afterwards. He said: 'It was a great round of golf – I played really, really well. I feel as though I've been hitting it well for the last couple weeks but I've just not really been getting much out of my game. But today I knocked a few putts in and gave myself plenty of chances. A bit disappointing bogeying the last, but 66 is still a great score out there and it puts me in a nice position going into tomorrow.

'I've just put a lot of work in. I struggled – I had a little bit of a back injury, which is still there, but it's getting a lot better. It'll probably take another two or three months to clear fully. But I feel as if I can swing with a lot more freedom and I can actually practise more, hit more balls and spend more time on the range, which has definitely helped. I put my old trusty putter back in the bag last night, which seemed to help. My putting was pretty good out there today.'

He said he was aware of the expectations and doubts over his form as a result of the blip – but was confident he was now back in a good place. Rory added: 'This year I got off to pretty much a perfect start for me. I spent the week in Dubai, practised really well, finished third in Abu Dhabi behind Martin Kaymer and Ian Poulter, and finished sixth in

Dubai. So my game was there, and then the back injury flared up during the last couple of rounds in Dubai.

'Since then it has been a little bit of a struggle. I'd get on the range and I'd hit balls and I'd maybe only hit 100 balls because I wasn't feeling very good, so I'd have to cut my session short and it's been like that for the last couple months. Ever since the Match Play this year, the whole season has been a bit stop-start so I'm trying to get a bit of continuity. I've added a couple of events to my schedule just to try and play a little bit more and to get a little bit of fluidity back into the season.'

He was also aware of just how close he had come to exiting the tournament after nearly missing the cut following a disappointing second round: 'I bogeyed the 6th to go to 3-over-par and I knew I needed to birdie two of the last three holes to make the cut. Luckily I eagled 7 – that could have been the turning point in the season. So, yes, I was very happy to make the cut and I'm happy with my round today. I made three bogeys so it could have been a little better but I'm very pleased.'

Ever the perfectionist, Rory continued to press on. After a good rest and relax on the Saturday night, he emerged fresh and determined to do business on the Sunday at Quail Hollow. He knew he had suddenly hit a purple patch and felt the tingle of excitement as he teed off. 'It was as if he had come through a heavy storm and was now walking in the sunshine,' a source said. 'The darkness and misery had gone and he really did believe that he could now pull off a minor miracle and win this tournament. He had the belief that his first PGA title was his for the taking, which is incredible given the problems with his back and the way his self-belief had taken a battering with those poor results after a good start to 2010.'

Rory had shot the lowest round on the Saturday and now did the same on the Sunday, carding a remarkable 10-under-par 62 to set a new course record and to win the crown that had looked only a pipedream as he struggled to make the cut on the Friday. His remarkable finale earned him a four-shot victory over Masters' champion Phil Mickelson – it was the last act of a stunning turnaround in fortunes. He finished on a total of 273, 15-under-par, and his efforts earned him a winner's cheque for $1.17 million.

Afterwards he explained how it all came about: 'It started on the range – I absolutely flushed it on the range. I went out there today and I was excited to play: I knew I would give it a good shot, I knew I was playing well. I just went out there and had no number in mind – I thought 10 was going to be a realistic target, but to go out there and – especially getting to 5-under-par for the round after 11 – I was in a pretty good position. Then to finish the round off like I did under that sort of pressure was very satisfying.'

Without sounding arrogant, Rory admitted that he had not been surprised to have done so well – he thought his form was turning for the better, that he was on the verge of something big. He said: 'I didn't feel a 62 was coming but I felt as if my game was definitely getting a lot better. The 66 yesterday was probably the worst I could have shot; I gave myself so many chances, I had five eagle putts. And then today I just carried on from there, hit some great shots and holed good putts to keep my momentum going.

'It seemed as if everything has just gone right these last two days. You get yourself into a mindset like that and you just keep going. I was walking off 11 tee and J.P., my caddie, said: "All right, let's try and get to 13-under." It's just been a great day. To go out there and make as many birdies as I did, given the way the golf course was set up, gave me a lot of confidence.'

He was asked to provide a little more explanation as to why he had shelved the idea of taking some time away from the sport and how he had motivated himself after feeling low. 'I got home and I took a few days off. I just said to myself, "Look, there's no point in feeling sorry for yourself here – you're not playing great, you need to go and work." I was hitting it well, and I felt as if all parts of my game were pretty good but it was putting it all together on the golf course,' he explained. 'So, last week, back home all I concentrated on was playing golf, playing with my buddies, playing with anyone, but just trying to go out there and shoot a score. I played Royal County Down on Thursday, Royal Portrush on Friday – and played pretty good at both. I shot 67 on Portrush on Friday, and I thought, well, if I can shoot 67 around here in a pretty good breeze, then I can shoot it anywhere.

'That was my mindset coming in here. I knew I was playing pretty good. To be honest, I didn't get much out of my rounds on Thursday and Friday, but obviously I made up for it on the weekend.'

And, finally, he touched upon that old cookie: expectation – and the fear it brought. He explained: 'Yeah, I definitely felt the expectation, though I had never felt it up until this year. I got myself into the Top 10 in the world. I felt as if I should be going out there competing in every event I played. I got to 7th in the world at the start of the year, so I was thinking, well, if I'm the seventh-best golfer in the world I should be going out and competing.

'I was putting a lot of pressure on myself, which you shouldn't. Sometimes you need to sit back and say, look, you're only 20, 21 years old, and you're doing pretty well, and just put things into perspective. I was probably trying to get to that point too soon – the way I was pushing and pushing – and it probably wasn't great for my game. After The Masters, I've just tried to free it all up, relax a little bit and just go out and play. And it's obviously worked this week – and hopefully I can have that same attitude going into the rest of the season.'

'I suppose I just got into the zone,' he added, saying the win was also an early birthday present (he would be 21 on the following Tuesday). 'I hadn't realised I was going in 9-, 10-under. I just know I got my nose in front and I was just trying to stay there.'

Inevitably, there were comparisons between himself and Tiger, who had shot 74-79 and went straight home without so much as an interview. Woods had been 20 years and 10 months when he won his first PGA Tour event in Las Vegas in 1996, a month younger than McIlroy. The respectful way Rory now talked about the disgraced legend spoke volumes for the young Irishman's character. Like Tiger, he was growing up in the spotlight but seemed an altogether more rounded, likeable individual than the man he himself had hero-worshipped. Rory said: 'I think I speak on behalf of all the early 20-somethings out here. Tiger was the guy that we all looked up to, and the guy that we followed and the guy that we turned on our TV for, and the guy that inspired us to go out to practice so hard. He was the person that set the benchmark so high. We want to achieve that [his level]. Even if we don't quite get to that level, it's still pretty good.'

So, Rory had won his first PGA tournament and now set himself another goal – to land that first Major. He knew it wouldn't be easy, that it would take dedication, concentration and hitting the sort of heights he had achieved in the last two days at the Quail Hollow. But he knew he would do it – it was just a matter of when.

CHAPTER 12

EASY RYDER

Just over 12 months on, Rory would land that oh-so important first Major – but there was still more learning and a lot of hard graft ahead. There would also be tears as he choked at The Masters. In this chapter we will examine his efforts up to the misery of The Masters in April 2011 – including his bow in the Ryder Cup.

He would show just how far he had progressed at The Open in July, held that year at the Old Course at St Andrews, Scotland. Rory had been singled out as one of the favourites for the tournament and lived up to the hype with a brilliant first-round 9-under-par 63 – two clear of South African Louis Oosthuizen and the lowest-ever first round score in the 150 years of the Championship, tying the course record.

Rory opened with an eagle on the 9th hole – and that

helped him grow in confidence. At the end of the first day, he was also four strokes ahead of Tiger Woods and three ahead of John Daly. Before teeing off, he had said he felt confident: 'I'm just really looking forward to the week. St Andrews at The Open is probably the biggest championship that we play and it only comes around every five years. There's a great atmosphere and a great buzz about the place. I'm pretty confident around this golf course. I feel as if I've played well here before, so hopefully it'll be a good week for me and if I can go into Thursday playing the way I have been the last couple weeks, there's no reason why I shouldn't be able to contend, come the weekend.

'The course is perfect. The condition of the place is really good. I played here Friday, Saturday last week, and it was a lot firmer on Friday. It rained a little bit on Saturday, which softened it up a little bit, but hopefully it won't rain too much on us and the course will continue to play nice and firm and fast.'

And after his magical first round, he told reporters at the post-round press conference: 'It went through my mind on 17 that 62 would have been the lowest round in a Major, that's probably why I missed the putt. But it was still a fantastic score. I didn't get off to a flying start – I was one-under through eight holes, and then the eagle on nine really turned things around for me and I just got going from there. It was great to get into the rhythm of the round and get into a flow.

'I think it probably is my most special [round ever] just because it's at St Andrews and it's The Open Championship.

But the 61 [at Portrush] was probably slightly better, if I'm honest. I don't know if it was because I was 16 or because – to shoot 61 around Portrush, especially the reputation that Portrush has [in Northern Ireland] – to shoot a score like that back home was pretty nice. But this is definitely up there. It's nice to put my name up there with the few guys that have shot 63 in Majors. It would have been lovely to shoot 62, but I can't really complain.' It seemed the rest of the cast would be playing catch-up with Rory over the weekend but a day of inclement weather on the Friday was to blow his hopes apart.

Rory had said how much he enjoyed the first round in the relatively mild conditions, but admitted he was aware this could change. He said he hoped it would stay 'the exact same as what I played in this morning,' adding, 'I've actually never played St Andrews when the weather has been really bad – that's probably why my scores have been quite good. I wouldn't mind the wind to blow a little bit, just so long as it stays dry, because I think this tournament – it's very special this year being at St Andrews, 150 years and everything – deserves a bit of good weather. I don't mind a bit of wind but as long as it stays nice and dry.'

But he would be cruelly out of luck, given the brilliance of that first day's play. With the same conditions as the Thursday, who's to say Rory wouldn't have gone on to snatch his first Major a year earlier than it would actually take him – in The Open, at St Andrews? Yet by the end of day two he was just grateful to have made the cut, such was the dramatic, bitter turnaround in his fortunes as he battled vainly for form in a howling wind that would lead to play being suspended for an hour.

Rory carded an 80 and with it an unwanted record – no player had ever shot such a high score after going so low the day before in a Major. He made the cut with his 1–under 143 total.

Naturally, he was in low spirits at the post-play press conference, admitting: 'It was just very, very difficult out there. I think all the guys were finding it tough and I just let it get away from me a little bit. I actually did well to par the last three holes – it could have been an 82 or an 83. I'm here for the weekend so it's not all bad, but definitely a complete contrast to what it was like yesterday.'

He was asked if the suspension of play after the first three holes had disrupted his rhythm: 'Yeah, I don't think they should have called us off the golf course. When we got back out there the conditions hadn't changed, the wind probably got a little bit worse. It probably wasn't a smart move.

'I felt as if I played the first three holes quite well, solid, and then I hit a good tee shot on 4, and then they called us in. It might have been a little bit to do with it – I'm not trying to make any excuses. Even from then I didn't hit it well and didn't put myself in the right places to try and make any birdies or make some sort of a score.'

But Rory being Rory, he was defiant – and said he still planned to 'have a go' for the rest of the weekend: 'There's a lot of big players that have missed the cut this weekend so at least I'm here for the weekend, which is a positive. It's going to be tough tomorrow. It all depends what the weather is like again. If the weather is calm, I feel as if I've got a chance to go make a few birdies again and go low. And if the weather is like this, the wind is like this again, you're relying on the leaders to sort of mess up a little bit because it's very hard to make ground when the wind is this strong.'

True to his word, he hit back on the Saturday, carding a 3-under-par 69 in the third round. That round – which included six birdies, a bogey and a double bogey at the 17th – put him 4-under but still miles behind leader Louis Oosthuizen, who was on 15-under. At least he was in a happier frame of mind as he spoke about the round – and the strength of character that enabled him to get back in business after his Friday nightmare. He revealed: 'I knew I was playing nicely – I'm not going to let one round of golf get me down. I really struggled yesterday but I think playing in such a strong wind yesterday made today feel not as bad, even though the wind was still quite strong. I definitely hit a few shots out there that I wasn't able to play yesterday. I think it might have just been because I had 80 shots yesterday, so I had a little bit of practice.'

And he still hadn't given up on the crown: 'If the lead tomorrow is 8-, 9-, 10-under-par going into tomorrow, I feel I've got a really good chance because I know what I'm capable of around this golf course and I know what I'm capable of in final rounds. We'll see how far off the lead I am and hopefully I [can] get off to a fast start.'

He was confident he could do just that and build on his third-round comeback: 'To shoot 69 out there is a pretty good score and to shoot 63 on the first day, I know what I'm capable of – I'll probably look back on the week and say, if I could have just made that 80 a 75 or whatever. We'll see what happens, but I'm still confident that I can go out and shoot a good one tomorrow.'

And the confidence wasn't misplaced for he would do just that on the Sunday at St Andrews with a final-round 68 and finish tied for 3rd, an excellent return considering his nightmare round of 80. As expected, Louis Oosthuizen lifted the claret jug, the South African finishing eight strokes ahead of Rory. Lee Westwood came 2nd, a shot ahead of Rory.

Generous in his praise for Oosthuizen, Rory said: 'Louis obviously got the best of it on Thursday and Friday and got to 12-under-par. You know, so he's 5-under for the weekend, which is still a great score. Louis has played so well and handled himself well under the pressure.

'I know Louis well. He played with me in the final round in Dubai last year and contended for much of that. We've all known he was a great player for a long time. I think he needed the win he got early on this season to give him a bit of confidence. He and his wife have just had a baby so he's in a good place right now. He's one of the nicest guys out there and everyone will be happy for him.'

Yet, inevitably, Rory was rueful that he had blown his own chances with that collapse on the Friday, admitting: 'If I had just stuck in a little more on Friday and held it together then it may have been a different story but I played really solidly in the other three rounds. After the round of 80 I felt I came back into it well by shooting 7-under at the weekend.

'My game is definitely there and I can take a lot of

positives from this week. I knew I had a chance coming here and it was nice to be leading for a while, but I'm still disappointed because I know if I'd played anywhere decent on Friday then I could have been contending for 2nd place at the very least. When you start a tournament by shooting 63, you fancy your chances over the next three days. It just so happened that it got very windy on Friday and I didn't play it well.

'It's always satisfying to be up there in a Major but in these circumstances, after starting so well, it's a bit disappointing that I didn't challenge a bit more. I don't know if I could have handled Friday a bit better; I had a day leading up to this week that was just as windy so I probably should have done better. I don't really count it as being on a learning curve. Major championships aren't won on days like that – they are won on days when you make birdies.

'It's not going to give me nightmares. I'm sure I will wake up tomorrow morning and see I shot 16-under for three rounds at St Andrews in The Open and had just one bad round. It's there for me to win. I knew I had a great record at this golf course. I love this place, it's my favourite course in the world – it's just a pity about Friday. I'm heading home tonight. Probably going to go up to Lough Erne on Tuesday evening, play the Lough Erne Challenge on Wednesday and have a relaxed weekend – I've got a new driver I have to test out as well. I didn't have it in the bag this week.'

The message was simple: it was business as usual despite the heartache of missing out on what could have been that first Major… and not just any Major, but The Open. And at least the tied 3rd finish had boosted his world ranking to an all-time high of 7th.

Next up was the 92nd US PGA Championship – he had tied for 3rd in his US PGA Championship debut in 2009 at Hazeltine National – and, as the scribblers kept pointing out, with it came Rory's last chance to lift a Major at a younger age than Tiger Woods. Yes, if he triumphed he would be one day younger than Tiger was when he won the 1997 Masters. It was not to be, but again Rory did well at Whistling Straits, particularly as he kept his concentration during the fog-hit opening two rounds. Padraig Harrington, Luke Donald and Justin Rose were among the big names to miss the cut. At the halfway stage, Rory was among the leading Europeans in a tie for 5th on 5-under with Simon Khan.

Rory said: 'I feel as if I'm in a really good position going into the weekend and I like the position I'm in. It's a nice place to be, I could make a charge.'

American Nick Watney led the field as they headed for Sunday's final round with a three-shot lead over Rory – who carded a 5-under-par 67 – and Dustin Johnson, so there was still a chance of Rory lifting the trophy. Watney doffed his hat to Rory and the other six under-30s (including himself) who were in the Top 10 on the leaderboard as they downed clubs on the Saturday. Watney, 29, said: 'I think that there's some really good players that haven't won a Major. And all the guys that have at one point they hadn't won either, so you got to start somewhere – and hopefully, tomorrow will be my day.'

Martin Kaymer, the 25-year-old from Germany who had

Above: Rory with Europe captain Colin Montgomerie and fellow Northern Irishman Darren Clarke at the 2010 Ryder Cup. The competition was held at Celtic Manor, Wales, for the first time.

Below: Rory in action during a Ryder Cup practice round.

Above: Rory and Graeme McDowell celebrate winning their Ryder Cup foursome match.

Below: Padraig Harrington, Graeme McDowell and Rory McIlroy with the Ryder Cup. Europe beat the USA 14 ½ to 13 ½ to clinch the trophy.

Above left: Rory is all smiles during the second round of the Alfred Dunhill Links Championship at St Andrews in October 2010.

Above right: Rory during a press conference ahead of the 2011 BMW PGA Championship Pro-Am competition at Wentworth.

Below left: Rory is a huge tennis fan and can often be seen at matches – here, he is pictured with Britain's Andy Murray and former Wimbledon champion John McEnroe during a visit to the All England Club in June 2011.

Below right: Considering his options during the 2011 US Open.

Above: Rory's father, Gerry, is a great supporter of his son – here, he is pictured watching the action during the third round of the US Open in June 2011.

Below left: Rory celebrates winning the US Open with his father.

Below right: Saluting the fans as US Open champion.

Above: Success at the US Open brought instant worldwide fame and recognition to Rory, making him one to watch in future tournaments.

Below left: Rory with the US Open trophy.

Below right: Rory follows his US Open victory with an appearance at the 140th Open Championship at Royal St George's, Kent, in July 2011.

Above: Rory during a practice round at the Open Championship, and (*above left*) with South Africa's Charl Schwarzer.

Below: Rory is mobbed by fans as he leaves the green after the final Open practice round.

Above left: Rory lining up his putt during the second round of the Open at Royal St George's. Unfortunately he struggled in difficult weather conditions as fellow countryman Darren Clarke lifted the claret jug.

Above right: The bad luck continued for Rory at the 2011 US PGA Championship, as he injured his wrist during the first round.

Below: Despite a valiant effort, Rory failed to make much of an impact in the competition as he tied for 64th place with Sean O'Hair, Peter Hanson and Padraig Harrington on +11.

Despite his struggles in 2011, Rory remains one of the brightest stars of the golfing world, and the future is sure to bring even greater success than he has already achieved.

won his fifth European Tour victory in Abu Dhabi earlier in 2010, said he was delighted that the 'kids' were making a breakthrough – and that he had been 'surprised at how aggressively his contemporaries are playing.' 'For example, Rory or Nick Watney, they go for every flag,' he said. 'So, OK, on this golf course you can be very aggressive because it's wet but it doesn't matter if you have a wedge or a 3-iron in your hands, they are always going for the flag. I think that's great, if you just accept and play shot for shot, and I think that's the way Tiger Woods plays as well. He always goes for birdies and I think that's a little bit the American style. It's awesome, it's great to see.'

Meanwhile, Rory had his own take on the rise of the youngsters, observing: 'I'm not sure if we're feeding off each other, I just think that we're all improving and we're all getting better every year. I definitely don't look at the young guys and go, "Right, I have to be as good as him" – I'm just trying to get better. And I think everyone else is sort of doing the same thing.

'I think the players are just getting so much better at a younger age. Their confidence is so high that they can take on shots that other guys just might not have thought they could. I don't know if that's because most of the guys swing it better out here now or whatever, but it does seem the younger guys are coming out fast and they're just a lot better and more ready to win.'

He also made it clear he would not be fazed by the way he lost out at The Open, indeed it would spur him on: 'I definitely have a chance and it is nice that it's come right after St Andrews. I realise I've got a good chance tomorrow and if I'm not too far behind Nick Watney.

'There's so many other great players on the leaderboard – someone's going to have to go out there and shoot a good score. It's nice to have another chance. I wasn't really in contention at St Andrews after the second day there; I did well to finish 3rd. And tomorrow I'm in contention in a Major, and it's a great place to be.'

He was indeed in contention but he could not muster up that little bit extra to win that year's US PGA. Rory three-putted the 15th green to fall out of a tie for the lead and his final-hole birdie putt narrowly missed the hole to leave him a shot away from the playoff between Bubba Watson and the eventual winner, Martin Kaymer. The Irish youngster was by no means disgraced, however – finishing tied for 3rd being of course his third top-three finish in a Major. He was playing consistently good golf and that elusive Major would surely come if he kept it up.

Afterwards, he was philosophical about finishing 3rd. 'I was just sort of always hanging around,' he admitted, 'and just waiting for that one putt to drop here or there. I got a good putt on 14 and I missed one on 15, which was quite disappointing. But it's been a good week – I'll take the positives from it. It wasn't the result that I wanted going into today, but it's a learning experience and hopefully one that I can establish myself for the next Majors.'

So, Rory would now head off on holiday thinking about another Major that had only got away by a small margin. He knew that he would now have to wait until the following year's Masters to try and win his maiden Major but he had a not too inconsiderable consolation awaiting him – a coveted spot in the Ryder Cup team of October 2010.

As excitement started to build for the event at the Celtic Manor Resort, near Newport, Rory would head to Wales with Team Europe. He was one of the 12-strong team skippered by Colin Montgomerie that also included Luke Donald, Ross Fisher, Peter Hanson, Padraig Harrington, Miguel Angel Jiménez, Martin Kaymer, Graeme McDowell, Edoardo Molinari, Francesco Molinari, Ian Poulter and Lee Westwood.

The Americans would be captained by Corey Pavin, with the 12-man line-up reading like this: Phil Mickelson, Hunter Mahan, Bubba Watson, Jim Furyk, Steve Stricker, Dustin Johnson, Jeff Overton, Matt Kuchar, Stewart Cink, Rickie Fowler, Zach Johnson and Tiger Woods.

As they arrived in Newport, Rory & Co. were in determined mood – keen to avenge the defeat by the US in 2008 and regain the trophy. Then, it had been held in Louisville, Kentucky and the US had emerged triumphant, a result of their own desire to win the trophy for the first time in this century – plus the blunders of Team Europe skipper Nick Faldo. The *Daily Mail*'s Derek Lawrenson succinctly pinpointed why the US had gone on to win 16½–11½: 'This was a Ryder Cup that will long be recalled for the blazing passion of a quartet of exciting American rookies and the desperate blundering of Europe's captain Nick Faldo.

'After almost a decade of American apathy, they didn't just win the Ryder Cup; they saved it. They were helped, alas, by some of the most incomprehensible decisions ever made by a European captain. It was bad enough that three classic fourballs players in Robert Karlsson, Paul Casey and Henrik Stenson never got a game in that format on the first day, contributing hugely to the early three-point deficit from which Europe never really recovered.

'What tied the noose around Faldo's reputation as a captain was the high-risk strategy of loading the bottom end of his singles order on Sunday with many of his best players.'

Team USA had ended their run of three successive victories for Team Europe, their largest margin of victory since 1981; it was also the first time since 1979 when the Americans had led after every session of play, with Faldo outfoxed by his US counterpart, Paul Azinger.

But there was little chance of Monty making similar mistakes in 2010. In many ways, this was the pinnacle of his career and he planned for the event in minute detail. 'He left nothing to chance, he knew preparation was key – and he proved a great captain, helping the younger players like Rory, encouraging them and keeping their spirits up, while also keeping his eye on tactics and how the event was progressing,' a source confirmed. 'He was excellent and deserved all the plaudits that came his way afterwards.'

Monty also had to deal with an imponderable – the good old British weather. It poured down on the first day and matches would have to be rescheduled after play was suspended.

Rory got off to a controversial start, claiming pre-tournament that Tiger had 'lost his aura.' He said: 'After what's happened in the last 18 months, I suppose a little bit of that aura is probably gone. Once I met Tiger, even before last year or whatever, you sort of realise that he is just a normal guy. He's probably the best player that's ever lived and likely the greatest player that's ever played the game.

'But you watch so much golf on TV, and you see so many things and you watch so many highlights – watching Tiger winning The Masters in '97 and winning four majors in a row in 2000/01, you sort of don't really believe it. You put him on such a high pedestal, and then you meet the guy and you realise that he's obviously an unbelievable player but he's just a normal guy.'

It was perhaps a provocative way to go into a tournament against the world's No. 1 – maybe even providing Woods with a much-needed incentive to do well. But Rory did not allow the controversy to affect him as play got underway.

In the opening fourballs he was paired with fellow countryman Graeme McDowell – and his showing certainly lifted the spirits of the Europeans. The match against Stewart Cink and Matt Kuchar had been hit by rain and when it resumed, they were 2-down with 7 to play. Rory showed his worth by hitting three birdies as he and Graeme halved. The display brought words of admiration from McDowell, who said: 'This guy was off the charts this morning, one of the greatest players in the world and one of the greatest players I've ever seen. We both struggled a little bit yesterday. With Rory's first experience of the atmosphere, it was very hard to get any kind of rhythm going then but he was unbelievable today. One of the keys to winning in the Ryder Cup is having a great partner. I've got one!'

Lavish praise indeed: Rory admitted he had been slightly overawed by the occasion as he found his feet on the first two days. 'It was unbelievable,' he said, commenting after the first day. 'I have never experienced anything like that at a golf tournament before. I was just happy to make contact with it down the first and had a good partner to rely on that won the first hole for us.

'I've played OK. I've hit some nice shots but it was so difficult the first few holes, and you know, even like I hit two great shots on the second and had a tricky little third shot, it was just made a lot trickier because the fairway was so wet and if you mis-hit it slightly, it can make you look very silly.'

Of course, he was much happier after his day two showing with Graeme and said he sometimes had to pinch himself to confirm he was here – that he had watched the event on TV since the age of six but actually playing was altogether a different deal: 'The real thing, it's certainly different,' he admitted, 'it's fantastic! Myself and Graeme said last night we didn't have any rhythm out there; I thought we did really well this morning to come back down from 2-down and grab a halve. We could have snuck a win at the last but I think we probably would have taken a halve on the 12th tee this morning. I'm very happy with how we came out and had a positive attitude out there. We just need to keep that going throughout the day.'

Europe won both the foursomes matches in Session Three to draw level at 6-6 and set up a tense finish. Lee Westwood and Luke Donald beat Tiger Woods and Steve Stricker 6&5, and then Rory and Graeme proved too strong for Zach

Johnson and Hunter Mahan, 2&1. Rory, who holed a birdie putt at the 17th to seal the victory, was overjoyed to chalk up his first win after halving one and losing one by a hole to Cink and Kuchar in the foursomes.

He said: 'Today felt great, to get that first win under my belt in The Ryder Cup is fantastic, and to do it alongside this guy [McDowell] is even more special. He's been great for me this week and he's made my life a lot easier, walking the fairways with him. It's been great.

'For me it's great to win a point but it's more important for the team. We are rallying today and we just really need to keep it going to win the first two matches and lead from the front. That's what we set out to do and we have been able to do it.'

He then paid tribute to McDowell (the man he dubbed G-Mac), saying the Irishman had been a major calming influence and had helped him no end: 'It's been great to play with G-Mac. At the start of the week, there was no one else I really wanted to play with. You know, he was the guy I wanted to partner. It was great to get three games with him. Even the match that we halved and the match we lost, the first couple of games, we both played very, very well. The team is great, but I just have felt more comfortable with G-Mac out there than I would anyone else. It's been fantastic so far. As Graeme said, to play with one of your best friends in The Ryder Cup is very, very special and hopefully we have a few more Ryder Cups in us and we can play alongside each other again.'

But now Rory was heading for the singles and would have

to cope on his own. Did that worry him? Not at all – 'I'm up for the singles tomorrow. It's going to be a great battle out there with whoever I'm playing, and it will be great to get out there and try and win a point for the team.'

For the first time in Ryder Cup history, the final session was played on the Monday after the torrential rain that had delayed the tournament on the first day. But it was another good day for Rory as he won a vital half point against Stewart Cink to help his team regain the Ryder Cup by a score of 14½ to 13½. Afterwards, the young Northern Irishman was delighted and said it 'had been the best week of my life' after mission accomplished, which had been 'to regain the Ryder Cup and bring it back to European soil, to do it for European golf and for Seve and for everyone involved.'

Indeed, when it was suggested that the experience would be good for him as he maintained his push to become the best player in the world, Rory sounded a little piqued. It wasn't about personal glory, he insisted, this was about the team: 'This isn't about me or the development of my career, this is about the guys that are sat in front of you here. It was a great match today with Stewart – he's played great this week. I've played against him three times this week and had three really good matches. He's just a gritty competitor – he holes putts when he needs to, he hits good shots when he needs to, and just doesn't really let you get away with anything.

'So, it was great to get a halve at the last and leaving my first bunker shot in there – yeah, it's fantastic. This experience this week has been so much different and so much better than any other experience I've felt at a golf tournament before. And you know, I truly believe that this is the best golf tournament in the world.'

And it wasn't just Rory who had been bowled over by the 2010 tournament. 'This is the greatest Ryder Cup ever witnessed on either side of the Atlantic,' declared Phil Weaver, chairman of the PGA, at the closing ceremony. 'The stunning atmosphere of The Twenty Ten Course has been challenged by the conditions but thanks to the good people of Wales, we have overcome.'

During his victory speech, Europe captain Monty added: 'This is the greatest moment of my golfing career. This was a showcase for European golf and it was a showcase for Wales, too. The standard of everything has risen to seven stars now.'

No wonder Rory was thrilled to have been a part of it. This was a truly magnificent, historic moment – but how do you follow something like that? Surely he would suffer a sense of anti-climax after playing in a world-class tournament such as the Ryder Cup when he was now forced to slog his way around the less-glamorous tournaments for months? Well, let's not forget he still had one ambition to realise: he had won a Euro Tour tournament, he had won a PGA tournament, he had played in the Ryder Cup – but his main dream had still not come true. As Rory McIlroy entered 2011, he was determined this would finally come about. Yes, he would win that elusive Major this year – and his first target would be The Masters in April.

CHAPTER 13

MASTERS MISERY

'This golf course can bait you into being too aggressive – that's what happened to Rory out there.'

Tiger Woods, Augusta, 10 April 2011

Ironically, given the misery and loss he felt after blowing up at The Masters of April 2011, this would ultimately be recognised as the tournament that defined Rory. OK, he would go on to win the US Open two months later, but the mighty triumph would always be overshadowed – and analysed – in the light of him turning adversity into glory after suffering at Augusta. Following this, he would forever be known as the boy-man who defied the odds and the despair to dig deep and come back bigger and better when it mattered.

Naturally, it was a devastating setback for the young

Irishman at the time, though. He had led for three days of the Major event only to 'choke' on the final one. Afterwards, he would not try to conceal his disappointment and pretend all was fine. Always straight and honest and ever-realistic, Rory simply admitted: 'I was still one shot ahead going into the 10th and then things went all pear-shaped after that. I'll get over it – I'll have plenty more chances, I know that.'

And he would add: 'I don't think I can put it down to anything else than part of the learning curve. Hopefully if I can get myself back into this position pretty soon, I will handle it a little bit better. It will be pretty tough for me for the next few days, but I will get over it – I will be fine. There are a lot worse things that can happen in your life. Shooting a bad score in the last round of a golf tournament is nothing in comparison to what other people go through.

'Getting applauded up onto the greens, I was almost a little embarrassed at some points but the support I had here was fantastic and I really appreciate it. I can't really put my finger on what went wrong – I lost a lot of confidence with my putting but I just hit a poor tee shot on 10 and sort of unravelled from there. I'll have plenty more chances, I know, and hopefully it will build a bit of character in me as well.'

That was the simple message for the massive gathering of press corps – highlighted by the brilliant line: 'There are a lot worse things that can happen in your life'. How true it is – and certainly for a boy from Northern Ireland, where The Troubles had cast a dark shadow over his birthland, where simply being alive and relatively happy was far more important than a round of golf, albeit at one of the world's top four tournaments.

Later, Rory would provide a more open analysis of the situation when he added on Twitter: 'Well that wasn't the plan! Found it tough going today, but you have to lose before you can win. This day will make me stronger in the end. Oh and congratulations Charl Schwartzel!! Great player and even better guy! Very happy for him and his family!'

If anything summed up the boy from Holywood, it was that simple, honest tweet. An admission that he just wasn't up to it on the day, but a vow that he would improve as a result of the experience – and a lovely tribute to the man who had stolen his glory. And the truth of it all was this: yes, he was right – he would improve as a result of the collapse, only even he could hardly have dreamt it would be so quickly down the road.

The final leaderboard at The Masters read like this: -14: C. Schwartzel (SA); -12: J. Day (Aus), A. Scott (Aus); -10: T. Woods (US), G. Ogilvy (Aus), L. Donald (Eng); -9: A. Cabrera (Arg). The Brits came home in this order: -5: J. Rose (Eng), L. Westwood (Eng); -4 R. McIlroy (NI); -3: M. Laird (Sco); -1: I. Poulter (Eng); +1: P. Casey (Eng).

The *Sun*'s David Facey best summed up the agony of Rory's display on that fateful final day at Augusta, saying, 'It was painful to watch, with the youngster from Northern Ireland crashing out of the lead in a flurry of horror shots. A triple-bogey, bogey, double-bogey run saw him unravel over a course that down the years has taken chunks out of some of the game's greatest players.

'And it was agonisingly reminiscent of Greg Norman's final-round collapse in 1996, which saw him surrender a six-shot lead with a 78. That allowed Nick Faldo to romp home by five shots, after shooting a closing 67.'

The *Daily Mail's* Derek Lawrenson urged readers to say a little prayer for Rory: 'In the entire history of major championship golf we've rarely witnessed anything like this. We've seen any number of players choke, we've witnessed plenty more simply not having the skills to cope with the suffocating demands of a Sunday afternoon. But has a man in a position to win ever suffered three holes to match those that befell poor Rory McIlroy in the final round of The Masters on Sunday? Amen Corner they call it, and everyone had better say a prayer for the young Northern Irishman after this disintegration.'

And Rory's local paper, the *Belfast Telegraph*, had this to say about his darkest day on the green: 'It was ecstasy for South African Charl Schwartzel in The Masters at Augusta today – and total unmitigated agony for Rory McIlroy. Schwartzel, 26, grabbed his first Major title after yet another amazing day of high drama that saw Tiger Woods charge into a share of the lead and McIlroy, four clear overnight, collapse to an 80.

'The 21-year-old's suffering was the biggest last-day collapse in a Major since Jean Van de Velde blew it from five clear at Carnoustie in 1999. Three years before that, of course, Greg Norman was six in front at Augusta and with a nightmare 78 lost by five to Nick Faldo. Now McIlroy's name will, for the time being at least, be grouped with theirs. He finished only 15th, an incredible 10 shots behind.'

Yes, it was that bad – Rory had now joined the likes of Van de Velde and Norman in the 'biggest chokers in golf' history books. So, how had it all gone down the pan after such a brilliant start? Well, let's rewind the tape to that first day at Augusta on a bright Thursday morning on 7 April. Rory had been working hard in preparation for the event and was confident he would be able to do himself justice. He did just that with a magnificent opening round 7-under-par 65 that left him joint top of the leaderboard with Spaniard Alvaro Quiros. Two behind in third were Koreans Y.E. Yang and K.J. Choi, while Tiger Woods hit a 71 to become joint 24th and defending champion (and favourite) Phil Mickelson with a 70 for joint 14th spot.

Rory's opening statement of intent brought back memories of his Major record-equalling first-round 63 in The Open at St Andrews of the previous July and he needed no reminding that he then went on to follow up with a soul-destroying 80. Now convinced he had the mettle to avoid such a demoralising repeat of fortune, he said: 'At the time it was very disappointing but looking back, it was probably very valuable in my progression as a golfer. I hope it will help me. I now have that experience to draw on, especially being in a similar position to last year at St Andrews. I feel like I'm better prepared to tee off in the second round of a Major with the lead. My start here was not as explosive or as spectacular as St Andrews, but it was very solid and it's a great start.

'I felt as if my game's been really good all season and after working on my game in Florida for 10 days with my coach,

Michael Bannon, I feel very comfortable. I'm still relatively inexperienced but I feel I am a pretty quick learner. There's no substitute for experience and I've still got a lot of learning to do, but I am getting there.

'It was nice to see a few putts drop in as well and hopefully I can build on it. I think what happened at St Andrews will be a massive help.'

Indeed it was a brilliant start at Augusta – the best, in fact, since Greg Norman's 63 of 1996. Rory was certainly far happier than some of the players predicted to be his biggest rivals for the tournament.

Mickelson, for instance, said: 'A 70 is just OK. I didn't shoot myself out of it, but I didn't make up the ground I wanted.' And Woods felt his game was picking up: 'We're in a Major championship and it's full systems go. I'm only 6 back.'

Lee Westwood – supposedly Rory's biggest challenger from back home – was concerned about his putting. He groaned: 'It's how my game is at the moment. If you can't hole it out from four feet, you're going to struggle, aren't you?'

Meanwhile, Rory kept his head while all those about him appeared to be losing theirs. On Friday's day two of proceedings he stayed calm and easily avoided a repeat of that nightmare 80 he carded at St Andrews. He hit a 69 to go 10-under-par and was now out on his own as leader in the tournament – two ahead of Aussie Jason Day.

But there was danger lurking as the Tiger advanced: Woods moved up to joint third after hitting a fine 66 to leave him 7-under. Tiger, who last won The Masters in

2005, warned: 'I'm right where I need to be. I kept staying patient, I was trying to get under par at the turn and piece together a good back nine and I got a bit hot. I closed the gap to three and hopefully, I can piece together another good round tomorrow.'

Mickelson was one-under but also issued a warning to Rory that he was gunning for him: 'These next two days are my favourite two days of the year, the weekend of The Masters. To be a couple under par, you can make up a lot of ground out here. I was able to do it last year on Saturday and I'm going to have to make a good run tomorrow, too.'

But Rory was not concerned about the rest – he knew success now depended solely upon his own game. If he could keep up the momentum, he would win his first Major, simple as that. He was pleased with his second day's work and that he was out in front, adding rather cheekily that, well, it was nothing new – well, was it? Rory said: 'I played the front nine really nicely. I didn't hole as many putts as I would have liked on the back nine, but I can't really complain – I'm in the lead going into the third round of The Masters. I've been in this position before at other Majors and I am relishing the fact I am in a good position again.'

Those were the words of a 21-year-old who knew he was good enough to win. Now all he had to do was keep his cool and not bottle it. Which he managed easily enough the next day, too.

On the Saturday he turned in another fine display to end with a 2-under-par round of 70 and a four-shot lead over 2009 Masters champ Angel Cabrera of Argentina, Charl

Schwartzel, K.J. Choi and Jason Day. Luke Donald (69) and Adam Scott of Australia (67) finished on 7-under, with Tiger Woods 5-under after a stuttering 74 and Mickelson 3-under with a 71.

Rory, who picked up three birdies in the final six holes, was delighted with his performance. His lead after 54 holes was the largest since Woods carved out a 9-stroke lead in 1997 – and ended up winning by 12. Rory said: 'That birdie at 17 was a bonus. I hit the putt perfectly where I lined it up. It was tracking the whole way and just dropped in the middle, it was great timing.

'I remember watching [Tiger in '97] with my dad. I was seven years old at the time. That's when Tiger sort of grabbed all our imaginations and broke so many records; it was a huge moment in the game of golf. It would be nice to get a Major early and show some of the young guys that it is possible, but we'll see what happens because four shots on this golf course isn't that much – there is still a lot of golf to play. I'm not going to think about anything but that first tee shot.

'It's a great position to be in. I stayed patient, I'm really happy with the way I stuck to my game plan and it paid off in the end. I feel comfortable with my game, with the way I've prepared and all of a sudden, I finally feel comfortable on this golf course.'

Rory told the press that he had been inspired by his pal Graeme McDowell, who had failed to make the cut and was urging him on. 'Actually he just texted me and told me he loves me – I don't know what that means,' said Rory, sharing a laugh with the army of golf hacks. 'I don't know if that's him or the beer talking!'

Rory was confident – and quite rightly so. He felt he had the taming of the course and his game had shown no sign of crashing. Indeed he appeared mentally, physically and emotionally ready and able to lay claim to his first Major crown.

Even the bookies believed he would now finish the job he had started. Betfair's Paul Krishnamurty explained why he was confident Rory would 'complete his masterclass', saying, 'Augusta has repeatedly proved itself to be a front-runner's course, with 19 of the last 20 winners coming from Sunday's final group. More importantly, what possible sign has there been of a McIlroy collapse? In truth, we should be grateful that his putting has been ordinary because Rory would otherwise be completely out of sight. The majesty of Rory's long game this week has been eerily reminiscent of Tiger Woods when he won his first Masters title in 1997. We may be witnessing a similar "changing of the guard".

'McIlroy looks so well suited to this layout that this may be the last opportunity for several years to back him at even money in a two-ball there. Having shown no weakness in the "bottle" department so far, I expect we'll see Rory cruise round today, playing conservatively while others struggle to play catch-up, before maximising the par-fives. I should point out that this doesn't suit my book, having already employed a successful trading strategy on Charl Schwartzel and backed Angel Cabrera at silly prices. If either man is to get close, however, I suspect they will have to shoot low rather than waiting for Rory to flounder. There's been precious little sign of it ever since he hit the front on Thursday.'

Few would have disagreed with Krishnamurty's assessment on Saturday night – and the prospects of a first-ever European Tour clean sweep of the Majors. The stark fact for Americans as they watched the contest unfold on their TV sets and at the course was that by the Sunday night, their country could be without the four Majors and the Ryder Cup for the first time in history. Certainly the threat of Mickelson would seem to have evaporated as he struggled to maintain contact with the leading pack on the Saturday – and Tiger knew it would take a miraculous final round for him to win. Woods said: 'I'm pleased with the way I played, but I just made nothing. I also had a couple of three-putts out there, so not very good. I'm going to have to put together a good front nine and see what happens.'

Meanwhile, the fans backed the idea that Tiger would not pull through and dominate on the Sunday; some questioned whether he would ever be as good as he once was. One fan, Michael, typified this view when he observed: 'The Tiger is a house cat. His domination is over and will never return. This guy pulled the wool over millions of fans as well as his adversaries on the PGA tour. So he gets a just reward. Be interesting to see what he does. But expect that his reign is over.'

Rory's army of supporters were confident he would finish the job at Augusta, though. One, James Edmonds, told me at the time: 'He has done so well over the first three days it would be a massive shock if he went and blew it now. He has looked cool and calm and has not let anything get to him. OK, he has made a couple of duff shots, but he never panicked when that happened. He just kept on, steady and certain as if he were playing towards a date with his destiny. He has managed to keep his rivals at bay and has continued to dominate them.

'If he keeps that strength and composure tomorrow, I'm convinced that he will lift his first Major. He has got the right attitude and a brilliant support around him with his dad and his management team, all he needs to do is keep on keeping on − and not let the pressure get to him. He can only lose to himself now…'

Prophetic words indeed.

The crowds had gathered in force to hail the new hero on the Sunday − some of the young Americans waiting 10 hours to get a glimpse of Rory. But many of them left early rather than watch him troop disconsolately back to the clubhouse after a nightmare final round. Rory had begun the day with a four-stroke lead and ended it ten strokes behind the victor Schwartzel, finishing a dreadful 15th. He made the history books for all the wrong reasons: his 80 round on the Sunday tied the worst final-round score by a 54-hole leader in the history of The Masters.

It was down to nerves and bad putting, as the *Belfast Telegraph* explained: 'Rory McIlroy missed a short putt at the first hole in the final round of The Masters and it set the tone for the day. On Thursday morning at the first three holes, his stroke was assured. The first real test came with a tricky par-putt at the seventh and in it went.

'His stroke was more tentative on Sunday. After the débâcle of the triple-bogey at the 10th, the weakness was cruelly exposed.'

Colin Montgomerie was one of the first Brit golfers to offer his commiserations – and to make it clear that this was not the end for Rory but merely the start of an era when he would lift the Majors. Monty said: 'He will have learnt from this experience. The next time he is in this position here – and it's a matter of "when", not "if" – he will pull through.' And Luke Donald, who tied for 4th, was just as sympathetic, saying: 'My heart goes out to Rory. When I saw he made triple on 10 and backed it up with a couple more tough holes on 11 and 12, I was gutted for him.'

Rory's fans were also convinced he would learn from this massive setback to re-emerge wiser and stronger. One of them, Terry, said: 'Rory, you have nothing to apologise for. The way you conducted yourself after your final round was a credit to you: you must have felt like running away but saw it through, unlike our petulant football managers who refuse to face the cameras after a match.

'Your time will come again – you have too much talent and a natural gift of being gracious in defeat. I feel certain that you have won a new army of fans both sides of the pond. You should feel proud to have led The Masters for 63 holes. Another opportunity will come soon. All the best.'

Diana, an American golf fan in Illinois, said: 'Watched the match on TV and CBS, mercifully, stopped showing Rory after he triple-bogied. I, for one, was rooting for him all the way, and was so sad to see the meltdown. I just keep hoping that his positive attitude will let him forget this misery and continue to play his magnificent golf.'

Meanwhile, back in Blighty, fan James Edmonds added: 'He's 21 and he will win this title in the future, no doubt about it. I know we're a nation of knockers, but isn't it time we actually got behind a young man who is so talented? If we support him and keep on encouraging him, he can only get better. Why is there a culture in Britain that demands we have to kick our sportsmen and women when they are down rather than give them credit for getting so close to pulling off unbelievable achievements, like Rory did? He'll be back and better than ever.'

There was something in what James had to say: although the majority of golfing enthusiasts were, quite rightly, supportive of Rory in his hour of need, some decided this was an opportune moment to put the proverbial boot in, accusing him of being a 'choker'.

One said: 'The curse of being a British sports star strikes again. The press big it up and then boom, it's the big flop! England football, cricket, Andy Murray, Rory, Henman – the only ones seemingly unaffected are the English rugby team.'

Another gloated: 'Can't imagine he'll ever recover from that, he's obviously a choker and as for saying there are worse things happening in the world, that's out of context and irrelevant; Majors won't be for Rory McIlroy but, eh, he'll earn a decent living and be successful.'

Even the august Business Insider website was caught up

with the 'Rory dilemma', asking if the youngster could recover from the setback, fretting: 'He can only get better, right? Or will he? There are plenty of young superstars who have showed the promise of a budding champion – some even won majors – but then disappeared. The truth is that you don't get a lot of chances to lead The Masters after 63 holes, and not every 21-year-old is equipped to handle such a devastating loss. McIlroy is doing OK, so far. Only time will tell if he can get back to the top.'

Rory himself, meanwhile, appeared before a plethora of media outlets and typically, was unwilling to make excuses. He told it as it was: he had thought he was on to a winner but it had all gone sour in that horror of a final round. As he laid the blame at his own door, he was honest and likeable – yes, he had lost his game after losing his nerve and no, it wasn't down to the course or the fact that he had a handful of the world's top players (including Woods) breathing down his neck as he started to crack up.

And as he kept on saying, South African Schwartzel deserved the fullest credit for keeping *his* nerve and winning the event – and let's not forget he was only four and a bit years older than Rory. For if there was one big positive to come from The Masters of 2011, it was surely for golf in general; that optimistic, fresh youth was making itself felt on the world's most prestigious greens at the world's most prestigious tournaments at a time when it was most needed after the dark cloud that descended over the sport with Tiger's descent into badness and madness.

Yes, Rory McIlroy was more than happy to doff his cap to

this ambitious fellow young golfer. Schwartzel had his hands on his first Major, but he himself would soon be following his example. Kevin Gartside, writing in the *Daily Telegraph* after The Masters, summed up the new era that was dawning in golf: 'This has been a tournament at which the New Generation has come of age. And what a generation. Charl Schwartzel, the exceptional champion, is just 26. Behind him on the leaderboard was Jason Day, who at 23 is only two years McIlroy's senior. Also on the course was Japanese supernova Ryo Ishikawa, a global star at 19, and poster boy Ricky Fowler, at 23 already a force in the game. Nick Watney, Dustin Johnson, Martin Laird, Alvaro Quiros and Gary Woodland were just some of the twenty-somethings launching rockets off the tee on the final day.'

Lifelong golfing fan Tony Woodward also applauded the way younger players now appeared to be grabbing the gauntlet at Majors: 'Probably the best Masters' finish I have ever seen. Certainly Rory did not hand it to Charles Schwartzel: he earned it as anyone having birdies on 15-16-17-18 deserves the recognition of winning a tournament. Hard luck for the Aussies though, but didn't they do well! Take heart, Rory – you have the talent and spirit to overcome this setback. Fantastic final day! Let's hope the rest of the PGA season is as good. The talent in world golf at the moment is amazing.'

Yes, it was true – the South African's win at the 75th Masters was no walk in the park despite Rory's collapse. He birdied the last four holes at Augusta to see off the challenge of Aussies Adam Scott and Jason Day by two strokes. It is worth noting that no Masters champion had ever finished with such a run – and Schwartzel had the added pressure of having to hold off 10 challengers, including Tiger Woods, as he attempted to keep his nerve and emerge triumphant.

Afterwards, the likeable Schwartzel said: 'It's a dream for me. It's such a special feeling, I just felt really comfortable. I've never been in a situation like that in a Major and I felt surprisingly very calm. It was just a phenomenal day. There were so many roars. The atmosphere out there was incredible.

'Adam Scott was making birdies and I needed to do something. I made some good iron shots and some good putts. From the word go on the first hole, things started going for me. It's always nice when things start in the right direction.

'Every single hole you walk down, someone has done something. I'd be lying if I said I wasn't looking at the leaderboard, but sometimes I would look at it and not register what I was looking at, and I think that sort of helped.'

The win in 2011 was all the more special for the South African as it came 50 years to the day after his countryman Gary Player became the first Masters' winner from outside America. 'I don't think I've ever done so much praying on a golf course in my life,' said Schwartzel. He also paid tribute to his fellow countryman Louis Oosthuizen, whom he said had inspired him at Congressional in winning the previous year's Open. 'To see Louis win The Open was just such a big inspiration,' he told the press corps at Bethesda. 'Just to see him do it made me realise that it is possible and it just took me over the barrier of thinking that a Major is too big for someone to win. We grew up together from a young age and we still play almost every single practice round together.

'We used to play every single team event, every tournament against each other and we represented South Africa for so long. We always travelled together, so we basically are the best of mates.'

And he sent his commiserations to Rory but stressed he was 'certain' that it would not be too long before the then 21-year-old would follow closely in his footsteps. He said he was delighted to have held his nerve, especially with the Tiger on his trail. For Woods, this was another disappointment as he tried desperately to put the furore over his private life behind him: he had now not won in 22 events, had not won The Masters since 2005 or indeed a Major since the US Open in 2008. Despite this, he claimed to be in good spirits: 'I got off to a nice start,' said Woods. 'On the back nine, I could have capitalised more. I hit it good all day – and I'm happy about that.'

Schwartzel would also later pay tribute to his father – which, with the benefit of hindsight, could be seen as a good omen for Rory, who was to do exactly the same when he came up trumps at the US Open. And the sentiments would almost echo his own, a couple of months later, as the South African said: 'My dad played such a big part in my golf and without him, I wouldn't have the golf swing I have or be where I am now.'

Rory was to remember those tender words when he spoke about his own father at Congressional but for now, he would have to lick his wounds and plan for the day when he too would win a Major. Plus, he had the benefit of an early chance to put the nightmare behind him in the Malaysian Open, which would begin soon after The Masters.

And there was one welcome surprise as he trudged back to the clubhouse at Augusta – his sweetheart, Holly Sweeney, was waiting for him. His management team had flown her in after he had taken the early initiative in The Masters, with the idea being that she would be there to throw her arms around him when he won the tournament. The *Sun* reported that she was kept out of sight for two days so that he would not become distracted as he went about his business.

In the end, she would provide a welcome shoulder to cry on for the young man, who buckled under the pressure. 'He was truly delighted to see her,' revealed a source. 'They hugged and it helped ease the disappointment for him – it was a lovely move by his managers.'

The young Northern Irishman with the world at his feet was once again ready to move: he now had four tournaments in which to get his game in shape before the next Major. Time to go back to work and to sort out both the psychological issues and the putting problems that had cost him so dearly in The Masters.

CHAPTER 14

PUTTING
THINGS RIGHT

He may have thought he had put the bad luck and bad fortune behind him, but Rory was to face an immediate double setback as he left America and headed for the four tournaments that would hopefully help him get his mindset and game back on track before June's US Open. Arriving at the airport for the flight to Kuala Lumpur and the Malaysian Open, he was confronted by a fellow passenger whose presence only served to rub in his Augustan nightmare – and when he landed in the hot, humid city, it was to learn that his golf clubs had gone missing.

At least the trip to Malaysia meant there was no time to mope or get too analytical about the unravelling at The Masters – not that Rory is that kind of character, anyway. He now turned his attention to those four events that would take him to Bethesda and the US Open: the Malaysian Masters, the Wells Fargo, the BMW PGA Championship and the Memorial.

For most people, though, it would have been a bit of a sickener to have to share a plane ride to the first of those tournaments with a certain someone who was probably the last man on earth he would have wanted to see after The Masters – yes, Charl Schwartzel! But Rory warmly shook hands with the new Masters' champion as they boarded the aircraft together and shared a joke with the South African. He even posed for a photograph with Schwartzel, who was wearing the winner's traditional Green Jacket from The Masters, on the flight to Malaysia. Later he posted the pic on Twitter, adding: 'Glad one of us has a green jacket on!!!'

Had Rory been tempted to try on the Green Jacket and have his own picture taken with it? 'No way was I putting on the Green Jacket!' he exclaimed. 'I'll wait to next year when, hopefully, I can get my hands on it.'

And he admitted that he was actually rather glad to see Schwartzel on the same flight – that the encounter had proved beneficial rather than detrimental. He said: 'Knowing Charl as well as I do has helped a little bit and if you look at all the current Major champions, I know them all so well. To see them as Major winners only tells me that if I keep doing the right things, it shouldn't be too far away for me.

'You can't take anything away from Charl after the way he played that last day. To go out there and start the way he did and then finish it off with four closing birdies was a great performance.'

Clearly he was already moving on and moving up – although he would suffer the further, more minor, setback of his clubs. When he arrived at Customs in Kuala Lumpur, he was none too happy to learn that they had gone missing in transit to Malaysia. 'It seemed to just about sum up Rory's luck,' said a source, 'but he didn't let any of it get him down. He's a naturally positive boy and he simply shrugged it off. It was no big deal in the scheme of things – they would eventually arrive later that same day.'

Rory himself insisted he had never had any intention of pulling out of the tournament in Kuala Lumpur – indeed, he confirmed that he thought it could be just what he needed after the heartache at The Masters. Upon arrival, he said: 'It was a long journey from Augusta, about 30 hours, but I'm looking forward to getting back on the saddle and putting last week's disappointment behind me. I've been excited about this event.

'Looking back on last week, I'm very disappointed. However, to sleep on the lead a couple of nights at The Masters and go into the final round leading was good. Last week, I played some of the best golf I've ever played. On Sunday, after one bad tee shot on 10, I just lost a bit of confidence. Those three holes really just killed me and then after 13, I knew I didn't have a chance. But for 63 holes I led the tournament and there are a lot of positives to take from it. Hopefully I'll learn from what happened on Sunday and it won't happen again.'

He was looking forward to making his debut at the Kuala Lumpur Golf & Country Club adding his only real worry was whether he would be able to deal with the high level of humidity. 'I can't wait to get out playing,' he said. 'My caddie has been out walking the course and I take a lot of positives from what happened in The Masters.'

It was revealed that he would tee off with two-times Malaysian Open champion Thongchai Jaidee of Thailand and World No. 1 Martin Kaymer. Schwartzel would be teeing off with fellow countryman Louis Oosthuizen and defending Malaysian champion Noh Seung-yul of South Korea. As he prepared to tee off, Rory received a tremendous boost from one of his heroes, Manchester United boss Sir Alex Ferguson. A big United fan, Rory was delighted to receive a series of texts from the Scotsman, encouraging him to move on from The Masters and backing him to recover from his upset and go on to triumph in tournaments galore. 'Rory was really chuffed to hear from Sir Alex,' said a source. 'He really respects him for all he has achieved in as many years at United as Rory has been alive – and he listens to him.'

Sir Alex himself later said: 'I really felt for the lad [at The Masters]. It was heartbreaking seeing him suffer, but there's no doubt he'll put what happened behind him because he's got real talent and the temperament to match. He'll have many more chances in major tournaments and it's only a matter of time before he wins them. He didn't need me to jolly him along, but I just wanted him to know that he has everybody at United behind him.'

It certainly seemed to inspire Rory as he carded a 3-under-69 in the first round on the Thursday in Kuala

Lumpur, five strokes behind leader Alexander Noren of Sweden, but four ahead of his Masters' conqueror Schwarzel.

It was good to see him smiling again after the first round as he told the press to stop worrying about him. Rory insisted: 'I'm fine – I think other people are more upset about it than me. I will have lots of other chances to win Majors. There are three left this year and hopefully I will have a great chance in all of them. The Masters was a little speed bump, but no more than that. The conditions here are very different from Augusta and considering I had not seen the course before, then I think 3-under is a pretty good score.'

Leader Noren also said it was good to have Rory back in business and admitted that while the Irishman had seemed fine, he himself had been a bundle of nerves before teeing off. The Swede revealed: 'I had two weeks off and I worked a lot harder on my game these two weeks than before. I was really nervous going into this round. I started off holing a nice putt on 10, 11 and 12 – my putter was great.

'After that my driver was steady then it was all about getting it close enough. I felt lucky at times when they kept rolling in, but you have to have that sometimes. I holed a lot from six or seven metres.'

He was also nervous that Rory was in his slipstream and sure enough, 24 hours later, his rival had caught him. In the rain-shortened second round, Rory hit an 8-under 64 to end the day tied with Noren on 11-under 133. Noren finished with a 69 as play was first delayed for three hours and then suspended while thunder and lightning added chaos to the proceedings.

Afterwards, Rory said: 'It helps when you have a morning tee time here as you are up pretty early. I went out and played well, and holed a couple of putts. I've been driving the ball pretty good, which you need to around here.'

A day later, on the Saturday, it got even better for Rory as he ended the third round with a two-stroke lead over the rest of the field. He managed just nine holes before a torrential downpour caused play to be abandoned. It meant that he led the field at 12-under-par after his ninth-hole birdie took him clear of Noren. Rory said: 'I felt I probably should have been a couple better. I hit a couple of good shots that if they went a foot either way would have been great – the tee shot on eight and second shot on six – if they had just stayed. But it's OK – it's a solid start. I could have been two or three shots better off, but it's obviously nice to hole that putt right at the end on the ninth and finish on a positive note.

'I've still got the lead but it is going to be a long day tomorrow. You've got to make every shot count out there. I've got myself into a good position going into tomorrow and that's all that counts. But 27 holes in that heat tomorrow is going to be tough.' And he wasn't wrong about that. Now the star that shone so brightly at The Masters before being eclipsed by self-doubt would once again suffer a final-day agony as he lost out on the Malaysian crown. Rory double-bogeyed the 12th and bogeyed two par-fives on his way to a 3-under 69. That left the door open for 17-year-old Italian

Matteo Manassero to clinch the title and the £255,000 first prize with a final-round 68 – which included a nine-iron eagle – to win his second European Tour title by one shot from French ace Gregory Bourdy.

Rory, who finished third two shots back, said: 'At this moment, I'm pretty disappointed. It's disappointing to lose for a second week in a row after giving myself another great chance for victory. I just misread the birdie putt at the last. It has been a tough two weeks and I'm looking forward to a break. Congratulations to Matteo – he's turning into one hell of a player.'

At least he had the consolation of earning a bigger cheque for his efforts in Kuala Lumpur than at Augusta – he received €108,349 for finishing third in the Malaysian Masters and $89,928 for his 15th place in the US Masters.

He now had a couple of weeks off to recharge his batteries, get in some practice and unwind a little back in Ulster with his family and girlfriend. But then it was off to the Wells Fargo Championship at the Quail Hollow Club, Charlotte, North Carolina. Yes, for his first appearance back in the States since that Masters' meltdown. And soon after arriving in North Carolina, Rory told the press pack that, yes, he felt better and was raring to go – but also that he had shared an interesting chat with the man who, 15 years earlier, had suffered a similar collapse at The Masters: Greg Norman.

Back then, Norman blew a six-shot advantage – and so Rory was interested to hear what the veteran had to say about how he had subsequently recovered and thrived. 'I had a good chat with Greg Norman the week after when

I was in Malaysia,' he revealed. 'He told me not to listen to you guys!'

Smiling, he continued: 'He sort of just said to me, from now on, don't read golf magazines, don't pick up papers, don't watch the Golf Channel. But it's hard not to — obviously you want to keep up to date with what's going on but you can't let other people sort of influence what you're thinking and what you should do. I've taken my own views from what happened a few weeks ago and moved on, and that's the most important thing.'

But what specifically had he learned from the meltdown? 'First thing, I don't think I was ready — that was the most important thing. I displayed a few weaknesses in my game that I need to work on, but I think you have to take the positives. For 63 holes, I led the golf tournament and it was just a bad back nine — a very bad back nine that sort of took the tournament away from me, I suppose. But what can you do? There's three more Majors this year and hopefully dozens more that I'll play in my career.'

Norman told the Australian Associated Press that he sympathised greatly with Rory: 'I knew exactly how he felt — I've experienced it. What is it with golf destiny? Isn't it strange? It taps you on the back of your head and it either pushes you ahead or pushes you back. What determines that? It's crazy.'

And then World No. 2 Martin Kaymer also had words of sympathy and encouragement for the youngster. He said: 'You know, he's only 21 years old and I think it's easy for people to forget — he's so young and the stuff that he did, the way he plays golf, it's been unbelievable. Yeah, he didn't play well the last round but that happens. He will win plenty of tournaments, maybe a few Majors.'

Those words were music to Rory's ears. Back as defending champion at the venue where he had won his first PGA Tour tournament 12 months earlier, he was feeling good – and determined to put the US Masters and Malaysian Masters last-day disappointments behind him. A year earlier, he had ended at 15-under-par 273 after making the cut on the number at one-over on the Friday and posted 16-under on the weekend. He shot a final-round, course record 10-under-par 62 as he beat Phil Mickelson by four strokes to triumph at the Quail Hollow.

This time around, he spent a little time with putting maestro Dave Stockton on the practice green before getting down to business. He had been concerned about his short putts and said Stockton's advice had been helpful: 'I just wanted to see him this week. My putting at Augusta, really the whole week at Augusta, wasn't what it should have been.' He added that Stockton had worked with him on his routine and how he should approach a putt – speed and delivery being key.

Rory celebrated his 22nd birthday a couple of days before teeing off at Quail, but the happy mood soon dissipated as he got off to a poor start at the event, carding a disappointing 3-over-par 75 to finish the first round 11 strokes behind leader Bill Haas of America. As he struggled to reach top form, he hit five bogies and two birdies, admitting: 'The story of the day for me was I just didn't hit it very well –

which is unlike me, being the strength of my game. My timing was off just a little bit.'

Haas had no such problems. 'I've got good feelings around this place,' he told www.pgatour.com. 'I'm comfortable, I guess, out there although the whole thing looks different with ropes and people and grandstands.' He said the fact that his putting had been spot-on had boosted his confidence – 'It makes you more comfortable over your iron shots knowing that you can maybe miss this shot and your putter might save you because I just had the good feelings going with it. It's early, and there's a lot of golf left to play, and I hope it can just work for some of that time.'

Rory too received a boost when he learned that he had overtaken Tiger Woods in the world rankings for the first time. He moved up to sixth from seventh, with the Tiger dropping from sixth to seventh. But that joy proved short-lived for he now failed to make the halfway cut as he defended his Wells Fargo crown. He missed out by three shots after hitting a level-par 72 – a round that included five birdies and five bogeys to finish 3-over.

Afterwards he was down but far from out, saying he would now get his head down and practise hard at home in Northern Ireland before heading off for the BMW PGA Championship at Wentworth. Rory said: 'I know better than most people that you just have to be around on the weekend to be able to make something happen. I was just trying to get in there, trying to get to the weekend but unfortunately I just wasn't able to do that.

'I'm disappointed to come back here after all that happened

last year and wanted to be here for the weekend. But that's golf, and I'll go home and I'll do some hard practice over the next 10 days, and try and get ready for the next event.'

Before Wentworth, he enjoyed a run-out in the sun at the Volvo World Matchplay tournament in Spain. Graeme McDowell beat Rory 3 and 2 to reach the quarter-finals of the event: a clash between Northern Ireland's two top players and one that seemed to bring out the best in McDowell. Beforehand, McDowell – who was ranked fifth in the world, one above Rory – admitted: 'He beats the crap out of me every time we play together, but this is the Northern Ireland match play championship and I'm hoping it's going to be different. It's the Volvo World Match Play and the pressure is on.

'I am sure he will expect to beat me, but it will be a great game and I am excited about it. He is a fabulous player, so talented. This course is all about driving the ball and he is pretty good at that. It's hard to play against a close friend but you've got to leave your friendship on the sidelines. I stopped playing him because he's too good. I'm more of an observer and he just tends to beat me up.'

This time, however, Graeme beat up Rory and afterwards Rory paid tribute to his good friend, saying he was 'a great player', although he added: 'I missed five chances in the middle that really cost me. It was a great battle but I couldn't get a putt to go in. I was getting very frustrated – when you are going against someone of that calibre you need to take your chances.'

After failing to make the cut at the Wells Fargo, Rory had

earned no prize money at all so it would be nice if he could clean up at the BMW. He also had some impetus to do well after watching Charl Schwartz earn the plaudits for his US Masters masterclass on stage at the European Tour's awards ceremony, two days before tee-off at Wentworth. 'It definitely hurt me a little bit,' Rory admitted. 'It's tough, but I'm a big boy and I'll get over it.'

But he wouldn't recover at the BMW. Once again, he was to struggle for consistency at a tournament, suffering an awful first round – making two birdies, three bogeys and two double bogeys for a 5-over-par 76. Rory was well off the pace over the next three days, too – with only moments of hope on the third day when he carded a 68. In between, he hit a 70 on the second day and a 73 on the final day as Luke Donald triumphed after a pulsating final-round battle with Lee Westwood. Rory finished tied 24th and took home a cheque for €44,100 – another disappointing weekend's work.

So, how was he going to raise his game in time for the next Major – the US Open, just over a fortnight away? Well, he had one final tournament to fine-tune and get into top gear: the Memorial in Ohio, which finished 11 days before the US Open would begin. It was his last chance to put down a marker before the big one and to show that, finally, he had blown away for good the cobwebs of despair from the US Masters.

And Rory got off to a flier as the Memorial got underway on Thursday, 2 June, ending up in the lead with Chris Riley after carding a 6-under-par round of 66 that included a flurry of late birdies. AP best summed up Rory's opening statement at the event, explaining just why he loved playing at the Memorial: 'Rory McIlroy only gets to play three regular PGA Tour events this year. He showed yesterday why the Memorial Tournament was one of them. On a Muirfield Village course that already ranks among his favorites, McIlroy had a birdie putt on his last eight holes and converted half of them on his way to a 6-under-par 66 to join Chris Riley in the lead after the first round in Dublin, Ohio. McIlroy hit the ball so pure that he shot 32 on the front nine despite missing three birdie putts inside 8 feet.'

Rory was delighted with his opening round, saying, 'That was a great way to start the tournament. Now I need to keep it up.'

His second-round effort wasn't as good but was still impressive. Rory would shoot a 72, but ended up three strokes behind new leader Steve Stricker, who posted an excellent 67 (after his opening 68). Stricker even managed a hole in one on the eighth and commented: 'It's a shock when you see that go in, obviously – but in a good way! It was a great way to finish the round.'

Rory's round included six birdies but he also had four bogeys and a double bogey on the 14th. He said he was angry with himself for 'making too many mistakes' – otherwise, 'I played good enough to shoot something in the 60s.' But he added: 'There's still a lot of golf left to play. I know that, and everyone else knows that. I just need to, as I said, just limit those mistakes. If I can keep the silly bogeys off the card, I think I'll be all right.'

Stricker stayed ahead of the chasing pack on the Saturday with another fine round, this time finishing with a 69. Rory, meanwhile, carded a 71 to sit on 209, five shots off the lead. It meant he was the only European in the Top 10 as the pack prepared for the final round in Ohio but he couldn't break the stranglehold established by Stricker. The American, who had never finished in the Top 10 in his 11 previous trips to Muirfield, closed with a 4-under-par 68 to win the event with a 16-under total of 272. Matt Kuchar and Brandt Jobe each carded a final-round 65 to tie for 2nd. Dustin Johnson also closed with a 65 to finish 4th, while Rory came home in 5th, with a final-round 68.

Rory declared himself 'pleased overall' with his display – and the $248,000 pay cheque for his efforts. He admitted he knew the final round would be tough, given he trailed Stricker by five, saying: 'You know you're going to have to do something pretty special.' But he certainly had a go and finished with an 11-ft birdie putt – which really boosted his confidence: 'It was a great way to finish the tournament. I felt as if I played really good this week – I just made a few too many mistakes, which really cost me and we'll have to try and cut those out before the US Open in a couple weeks' time, but there's definitely a lot of positives to take from how I've played this week.

'I feel as if I drove the ball really good, putted the ball really good this week. My game is in good shape, I feel really good about it. My putting has been very solid the whole week, so you know, that's a huge positive to take into the US Open. If anything, just a little bit of strategy more than anything else, just if you're going to miss shots, miss it in the right places.

'This week, if you miss greens it's very penal here and you get punished quite easily. It's the same as the US Open: if you miss it in the wrong places, you're looking at a 5 or a 6 so it's just something I need to address a little bit.'

They were the words of a man who was starting to feel confident again. Slowly but surely, he was on the up after the devastating down of that US Masters' collapse. He was feeling his way back to form, rebuilding his confidence and improving on his putting technique, thanks to the session with Dave Stockton. The tide was turning his way; he felt it. He knew that if he kept on this way he would be ready for Congressional – and ready to put the nightmare of Augusta to bed, once and for all.

'He had been working so hard in practice and on the greens,' a source confirmed. 'It was hard work but he was determined to be ready when the US Open came around – that had always been the plan since the US Masters ended. OK, he hadn't won any of the tournaments after Augusta, but he had been using them to fine-tune his game and rebuild his confidence. By the time he left Ohio for Haiti on the Monday, he was confident it had worked – and that he could show his true worth at the US Open. He was a man on a mission: to win at Congressional; everything, every minute since Augusta had been building up to that.'

First, he had another mission to complete: the one that took him to Haiti as an ambassador for UNICEF. It was a cause close to his heart – to help and inspire others less fortunate than himself. He in turn was to be inspired by the trip and the kids he would meet out there; they would cast a powerful, positive shadow over his work at Congressional. After a couple of days in Haiti, he would return to America and get down to serious business – playing several practice rounds at Congressional in advance of the US Open. For the wonderboy from Northern Ireland, the moment of destiny was nigh.

CHAPTER 15

RORY, RORY, HALLELUJAH!

After he won the US Open, the world would go Rory McIlroy crazy. Almost overnight, he became an international sporting superstar. He would be in demand for talk shows, sponsorship events, fan events, Wimbledon, world boxing fights – even pop stars wanted to be seen with him – and he in turn would lap it all up. After the disappointment and misery brought on by his collapse in The Masters, you could hardly blame him for taking time out to celebrate such a sweet victory. He had come a long way from Augusta to Congressional, had worked so hard to sort out his game and his mental outlook – little wonder that he now unwound for two of the three weeks before the next big challenge: The Open at St George's.

No one could deny that he had earned it.

Both the fans and the pundits were united in their belief that Rory's win marked a turning point in golf – that it was a case of out with the old (Tiger) and in with the new. And that he had actually come to the rescue – as a saviour-like figure – at the very moment golf needed one.

In an editorial, Belfast's *Sunday Life* magazine even argued that the boy had now earned the right to be known simply as 'Rory' – as, say, David Bowie was universally dubbed 'Bowie' – given his exploits at Congressional: 'Everybody knows that Rory McIlroy brought back a lot more from America last week than what he left with. But, amidst all the drama, hysteria and sustained celebrations, there was one significant thing he forgot to pack. His surname.

'Doesn't need it any more, you see. From now on, Rory is well, just Rory.

'Those four unrelentingly brilliant days at Congressional gained the 22-year-old membership of the golf world's most exclusive body – the "one-name club". Precious few occupy its hallowed premises; Arnold, Jack, Seve, Tiger. And membership will be officially confirmed at The Open in Sandwich next month when Peter Alliss announces: "there's Rory on the 11th fairway…"'

Then there were those pundits who were out to show how Rory had made golfing 'cool' once again after the fallout over Tiger's affairs – how he had indeed saved the day for the sport.

Writer Kolby Solinsky of Huffpost Canada perhaps best summarised the effect of Rory as 'saviour' when he commented: 'In winning last weekend's US Open, Rory

McIlroy proved what golf enthusiasts, club pros and the occasionally overweight gentleman in a pair of chinos and a Tommy Bahama fedora have been pledging for decades: golf, for lack of a better word, is cool.

'McIlroy is an undoubted light at the end of the Tiger tunnel, a tunnel that featured a stunning car crash and severe highway traffic. Tiger's exodus – not from the game, but from that lofty throne in the clouds where Zeus and Hera live – left the game he helped build in an almost heart-stopping turmoil.

'You could have tried the defibrillators, but it looked like golf was dead. I know that Rory's great. I know he's talented, and he's charismatic and – here's that word again – "cool".

'But, McIlroy is not here to replace Tiger's records (or, future records). He's not here to take his place on the tee. He's not here to be Tiger. He's here to show that golf is alive and well, and that it isn't just surviving without Tiger winning every tournament – it's better.'

It was an uplifting observation, as was the comment in the *Daily Star* that Rory's Congressional win had been akin to a sporting miracle: 'Rory McIlroy's superhuman-like slaughter of the US Open course and field was a wonder to watch. Not only did Rory McIlroy rip up record books left, right and centre with his amazing 16-under-par score. He also annihilated a world-class field by finishing eight shots clear. It's hard to put McIlroy's masterclass into proper sporting perspective. But it's akin to a tennis player winning the Wimbledon men's singles final 6-0 6-0 6-0. Comparable to winning the men's New York Marathon by 30 minutes. Or knocking out the world heavyweight champ in the first round. And what made it even more amazing is that the Ulsterman made a procession of Congressional after his last-day disasters at The Masters.

'To come back so soon and so strongly after Augusta when he crashed and burned so horribly on the back nine is, perhaps, his greatest triumph.'

Meanwhile, Rory himself was more concerned at that particular time with savouring his US Open victory than worrying about how he would go down in the record books and how he might be viewed as a potential saviour of a sport that had lost a good deal of its gloss. Yes, the Northern Irish lad now celebrated with a vengeance – and no one begrudged him his moment of letting his (curly) hair down.

Indeed, for days after his momentous win the tributes continued to pour in from fellow golfers and fans alike. 'Better than Tiger Woods at the same age,' was former Open champion Mark O'Meara's verdict. And 2006 US Open champion, the Australian Geoff Ogilvy, was just as generous in his praise – 'Rory is by far the best young player I've ever played with' – while US star Ernie Els summed up most people's belief with the words: 'The next No. 1.'

Phil Mickelson, who had won five Majors in his career, voiced the opinion that Rory was right up there *now*. The American, who played the first two rounds with Rory at Congressional, said: 'Rory played some really terrific golf. He hit the ball well and rolled it well on the greens so it was inevitable he was going to make some birdies. It's pretty cool. I could tell that Rory has had this type of talent in him for some time now and to see him putting it together is pretty neat to see.'

World No. 1 Luke Donald was just as complimentary. The Englishman joked that he 'was thinking about moving to Northern Ireland' and added, 'This will have a huge influence on the game. As I've said before, Rory has probably the most talent I've ever seen in a golfer – it's lovely to watch him play. He has such a fluid motion and he hits it far. He's got a great attitude, on and off the golf course, and he has no fear. He's not quite dominating the game yet but a win like this will do wonders for his self-esteem.'

Lee Westwood, meanwhile, admitted that he had been inspired by Rory's win to himself go out and steal a Major. The 38-year-old had still not claimed one of the four Majors but he told the *Daily Telegraph*: 'I know that if I play well enough, I'm capable of beating anybody. If anything, it's a confidence boost to me. Rory has obviously looked at us [senior figures at ISM, including Darren Clarke and Ernie Els] and learned how to be professional, and I can look at him and see how it is to win a Major. He won it in style. It is in the back of your mind that if Rory can win like that then so can I – I need my good golf to be better.'

And Rory's former playing partner Lloyd Saltman was another inspired by his success at Congressional. Just days after that win, Saltman, 25, shot a 6-under-par 66 in the BMW International at Munich to claim a share of 9th place beside fellow Scot Paul Lawrie on 137 – just three shots off the pace.

Saltman played in the 2007 Walker Cup team with Rory

and the pair have become firm friends. He said: 'It really inspires me seeing the guys from that Walker Cup squad doing well and watching Rory gave me a real lift coming here this week. He did something special in taking the US Open and it just puts into perspective how achievable winning tournaments really is. I sent Rory a text message to say well done and I was so pleased to watch the way he played the last round.

'His win has given me a lot of belief as I now know people who were on the same Amateur team as me in 2007 can go on and win a Major. And Rory did not just win a Major – he blew the field away!'

Even Charl Schwartzel, who took advantage of Rory's collapse at The Masters to win that tournament, expressed his delight that his friend on the circuit had now put things right in the US Open. He said: 'It's pretty spectacular what he's done – it looked like he was playing a different course.'

Rory's growing army of fans was equally impressed and also felt they had witnessed the changing of the guard at the top of the world golfing order. One, Dave D, said: 'I recall when Bob Dylan wrote "The Times, They are a Changin'" – yep, Rory is only 22. Tiger is 35. Oops! I mean, "Tiger who"?'

And readers of the *New York Times* were not immune to the delights of the dawn of the McIlroy era either. In a letter to the sports editor, Barry Herman said: 'The unquenchable thirst for sports heroes was never more evident than at the United States Open and the impressive victory of Rory McIlroy.

'With his image shattered, Tiger Woods has been forever replaced by the young, likable McIlroy. Even the commentators and fellow golfers ignored Woods as inevitable comparisons were pronounced: the flawless swing of Snead, the masterful flair of Ballesteros and the bright future of Nicklaus.

'No sports figure can ever really match an idealized persona. Let's hope that McIlroy can come closer than Woods.'

Back in the UK, another fan – John Fitz – commented: 'I was never really interested in golf until now. I thought it was a rich man's game, a posh man's hobby, but that has all changed now. Rory has shown that normal people can play it and enjoy it – and suddenly it seems much more hip and desirable. I am planning to buy some clubs and have a few lessons with the pro at our local golf club. Thanks for the tip, Rory!' And another, James Edmonds, said: 'I think it's brilliant what Rory McIlroy has done with his win at the US Open. I am a long-time fan of golf but reckon Rory's success will boost the sport and encourage many to take it up – a bit like Lewis Hamilton's success back in 2007 gave F1 a real boost and led to many youngsters taking up karting. Rory, you are a hero and a legend! I salute you!'

That idea was reinforced after Rory's win when youngsters near Liverpool took part in a nine-hole event at Aintree Golf Course as part of a nationally organised competition. The players – some aged only eight – were said to have been inspired by Rory and keen to emulate his success in the inaugural Junior Trailblazer Tour event. And then it was the turn of the North East to benefit from the buzz created by Rory as Hartlepool College of Further Education announced that it was to start a golfing academy in a bid to support the stars of the future. The new partnership between the Stockton Street College and Seaton Carew Golf Club was the first of its kind in the region.

Rory was obviously trailblazing a path that other kids were now eager to follow. American marketing executive Elisa Gaudet had noted the phenomenon while attending Congressional. Writing for the US website Cyberspace, she observed: 'As I sat sipping espresso from my newly purchased 2011 US Open Congressional coffee mug I can't help but think how it is the perfect symbol of what is currently going on in golf. A little bit of European mixed with a little bit of American and a whole lot of hope. After Rory McIlroy's resounding US Open victory two weeks [ago], I felt a new sense for golf – hope. The US Open Congressional looked more like a Justin Bieber concert than a golf tournament because of the number of teenagers in attendance.'

Rory had become a flag bearer for the next generation, someone they could relate to and someone they wanted to follow – a truly international hero and his fans would prove loyal to the cause. Bob Blubaugh, of America's *Carroll County Times*, noted how devoted those fans had been during the Congressional win: 'Rory McIlroy hadn't even reached the first tee Saturday when the infatuated cheering began. The first impromptu chant of "Let's go, Rory!" began after his tee shot at the second. After an errant drive on No. 3, a male, twenty-something fan lamented that the ball hadn't hit him in the chest: "Right on the nipple, I wouldn't care." Throughout the entire third round of the US Open at Congressional Country Club on Saturday, fans rained enthusiastic support upon the 22-year-old Irishman.

"'It was incredible, just fantastic," said McIlroy, who takes an eight-stroke lead into today's final round. "It's nice when you get a standing ovation nearly every green.'"

And if they were keen to show their ever-growing appreciation in the United States, the fans back home in Northern Ireland were an even more devoted bunch. Certainly, they turned out in force when the youngster returned after his triumph. They greeted him when he landed at George Best International airport and the banners were out in force as the local hero returned to his native Holywood. 'Congratulations Rory, Major No. 1' proclaimed one en route as he was driven into his hometown. 'Holywood, proud to be the home of Rory McIlroy,' said another. Then it was on to Holywood Golf Club, where dozens awaited the arrival of the young man who had put the town on the map.

His father Gerry was already on the premises to meet and greet, while the fans clapped and cheered when 22-year-old Rory emerged on the clubhouse balcony with the impressive silver trophy he had clinched at Congressional. 'It's great to be home – and even better to be here with this trophy!' he told the faithful. 'This is a great time for Irish, British and European golf.' He did seem a little overawed by the mass of journalists and photographers who had gathered to take note of his return home, though. It was at this moment, I am told by a source close to Rory, that he finally realised the full impact of his win on his life and his community. 'It was the moment he became an international superstar,' said the source, 'there would be no hiding place now – he was no longer the sole property of Holywood, Northern Ireland. No, he had become the hero and role model for thousands worldwide. His life would never be the same again – and he knew it.'

He did try to play down the adulation, however, saying: 'I'm going to do my best to be the same Rory I was when I turned pro in 2007.' His long-time girlfriend Holly Sweeney, who was studying sports technology at the University of Ulster, certainly intended to make sure he kept his feet on the ground. When he had arrived home as a hero she had hugged and kissed him, then told him to get his dirty clothes out of his suitcase as she was about to put on a wash! He might be the big star away from home but back home, he was just her Rory.

At the time, Rory made it clear that he owed a big debt of gratitude to Holly for her unflinching support as he marched towards the big time. He said: 'Holly and I have been together since I had just turned 16 and she was 14. She knows me better than basically anyone else in this world does, apart from my parents. And to have someone like that with you is very grounding.'

He revealed that they had met on a golf course when they were teenagers and separated briefly at the start of 2011, but got back together soon afterwards as they had missed each other too much. 'I thought I wanted to focus on my game and take a break or whatever, but I realised pretty quickly I'd made a mistake. And I had to do quite a lot of begging and grovelling to get her back!' he admitted.

In an interview aired on the BBC after the US Open win, Holly, 20, revealed the time apart made them realise they had made a mistake in splitting. She said: 'It was always going to be tough to take a break from each other. We both decided to do our own thing. I needed to step it up with uni and he needed to do his own thing with golf. We just needed to take a bit of time and realise what he needed to do.'

Rory said at the time that Holly was his soulmate as well as his lover: 'She's obviously my girlfriend, but she's also become my best friend over the past few years. I can say things to her that I wouldn't be able to say to anyone else.' He also conceded that being with Holly is also the main reason why he did not join the PGA Tour: he won his first PGA title at Wells Fargo Championship at Quail Hollow in 2010 but did not want to spend too much time in America away from his girl. Of course if he changed his mind, he would be able to join the Tour whenever he wished. His US Open win meant he earned a five-year exemption to do so.

The idea that Rory would stay grounded was reinforced the very night after the reception at Holywood Golf Club. There was no slap-up champagne bash at a smart restaurant – no, Rory, Holly and the rest of the family tucked into a Chinese takeaway while watching the TV, with Rory plumping for his usual favourite: a chilli chicken with honey stir-fry. 'All the family were determined that life should continue, as far as was possible, to be as normal as possible,' a source explained. 'No one expected success to go to Rory's head, and it won't. He's simply not interested in being the big star or having the flashiest material things – he is happy with a nice comfortable life, being with his family, and playing his golf. That's it.'

Maybe so, but it didn't stop Rory veering slightly off that straight and narrow path over the next few days. He even partied with JLS. The boy-band had been impressed by his Bethesda win and sent him a message of congratulations which, in turn, led Rory to invite them to his house.

So it was that the band – Aston, Marvin, JB and Oritise – visited Rory at home and made plans to hit the town. 'The JLS lads have become big golf fans and Rory is their hero,' a source said. 'They had a laugh at Rory's house on Friday and on Saturday, got together for a tear-up in Belfast. They also set Rory up in a box for their gig at the Odyssey. The Saturdays and Alexandra Burke were also in the city, so they all ended up out together after the gig.'

It was then revealed that Rory had even become the subject of a new song – not by the likes of multi-million selling artists such as JLS, mind you. No, he had been honoured by Irish band The Corrigan Brothers, who had a big hit on YouTube with 'There's no one as Irish as Barack Obama'.

Their new number, 'Rory McIlroy: US Open Champion Song' – was in homage to their hero. Love it or hate it, you can't deny the heartfelt admiration.

Rory is, as we have noted, a big Manchester United fan but he also loves boxing, tennis, indeed many sports. After his return home, he headed off to Wimbledon to cheer on Andy

Murray from the Royal Box and then took a flight to Hamburg in Germany to witness the David Haye-Wladimir Klitschko world heavyweight fight.

Rory arrived at Wimbledon on Tuesday, 28 June and was given a hero's welcome as he entered the Royal Box for the Ladies' Quarter-finals. He also met up with Andy Murray and another of his favourite tennis idols over the years, John McEnroe.

Murray would pay tribute to Rory's Congressional achievement but contended that it would be hard to compare their relative feats: 'It's just different. They're very different sports in many ways, tennis and golf, because you're always sort of in control, I think, in golf. In tennis, like [against Gimeno-Traver], the first set and a half, I wasn't in control of what was going on out there so they're very different. But the way that he came back from what happened, of having a chance of winning his first Major, was great.

'The way he dealt with everything was fantastic. The way he responded from the lead that he had earlier in the year was excellent. He's going to probably go on to be one of the best golfers that we've seen, I think.'

Those were generous comments – especially when you consider that Murray's nemesis, Rafa Nadal, the world's No. 1 tennis star, is a very good friend of Rory's. In turn, Rory repaid the compliments – saying he believed Murray, who had lost in three Grand Slam finals, could take heart from his own endeavours in transforming his fortunes and win Wimbledon: 'I would love to see Andy win his first Grand

Slam. I can relate to him on how much pressure there must be on him from everyone. He's come close before, too – winning three times. So it would be great to see him do it. Once you get that first one out of the way, you'll think things will start happening for you. To win his first one would be great for British tennis and British sport in general.'

He added: 'It would be great if Rafa won, but I would really like Andy to get his first slam at Wimbledon this year. Nadal was one of the first people to get in touch after I won the US Open. He texted me a "well done" – his text messages make me laugh because they are just like the way he speaks. They are in broken English, which is quite funny. He said: "You're the champion, you're the best all week" and he added that he was very happy for me.

'But I think, with Andy, that winning your first one definitely makes it easier to win more. It is a big hurdle to get over. Once Andy can win his first one, he'll be off and running. I think that clearly he can do this. I am a big follower of tennis and he can hit some shots and cover the court like other players can't.'

Of course, if Murray did win Wimbledon he would also likely lift the BBC Sports Personality of the Year award – at Rory's expense. Not that this worried the boy wonder. When told of the possible outcome, Rory merely shrugged his shoulders. 'He is not a boy who envies others or wants to prosper at their expense,' I was told. 'If Murray did win that award, he would be really happy for him. He just accepts things and moves on – always has and always will. That is his make-up, he is a genuinely nice, easy-going guy.'

Murray, on the other hand, accepted that he would need to win Wimbledon if he were to beat Rory to the title. He said: 'I have not been to Sports Personality for a few years now as I have been training over in Miami, but a few people have said to me that because of what Rory has done, unless I win this week, I have got no chance! I think it's great the way he dealt with everything after he'd obviously got nervous earlier in the year at The Masters.'

The Scotsman, who says he is a 15-handicap, added: 'I do play from time to time, but haven't for about a year now because it's quite a strain on the back. I have not lost a game of golf for five years, though I'm not great. If you think I get frustrated on the tennis court, you should see me on a golf course! I'm sure I'll give it more of a go when I'm older – everyone does – but I'll stick to the tennis for now.'

As July loomed, it was announced that Rory would appear on the CNN chat show, *Piers Morgan Tonight* – a sure a sign as any that he was now a worldwide name. The presenter himself was more excited than Rory that the boy was to be on his show, announcing on Twitter: 'BIG NEWS: I just landed 1st excl interview with @McIlroyRory + he's going to give me a golf lesson and we'll drink Guinness. #BackOfTheHole.'

And there was still more excitement when it was then announced that after The Open in Kent, Rory would be heading back across the Irish Sea to be the headline act at the Irish Open at the end of July. European Tour chief executive George O'Grady took the hype surrounding the youngster to a completely new level when he told the *Belfast*

Telegraph that Rory was the 'Elvis Presley' of professional golf! O'Grady outlined a series of extra security measures that would be put in operation for the Irish Open – precisely because of the ever-growing clamour surrounding the youngster. He said there would be Ryder Cup-style crowd safety measures to cope with a crowd at the Killen Course expected to surpass the 80,000-plus who had attended the previous year's event, adding that it was all because of Rory's personality – that people wanted to come and greet the 'People's Champion'.

O'Grady said: 'Wherever he goes in Ireland, Rory is everyone's pal. So we'll have to introduce crowd control, a bit more like the Ryder Cup with wider walkways because you are dealing with something like the Tiger Woods' effect. If it's all too tight, everybody will want to shake Rory's hand and he probably would shake everybody's hand but he's also got a championship to play.

'We'll also have to look at autograph policies and other measures to ensure Rory's comfort and safety as he plays and that of the spectators. This kid is a superstar – it's because of the way he conducts himself, how he responded to what happened in Augusta and how he treats people in general.

'For example, Rory must have been knackered after a day's filming with one of his sponsors at Wentworth on Monday, but still stuck his head around the door at the Tour offices. He said hello to the staff and signed autographs, chatted with the girls and happily posed for photos. This is Elvis Presley sort of stuff!'

Yes, Rory was becoming a worldwide superstar – the

bandwagon was rolling at a mighty pace and there was no stopping it now. His down-to-earth personality and sporting genius was bringing golf back into fashion after its eclipse coinciding with the fall of Tiger. But the beauty of Rory was that for all the acclaim, adulation and fame, he remained the same lovely guy from Holywood, NI: he refused to be swayed by the bullshit and false gods of celebrity. He knew where his roots lay and that his prime responsibilities remained with his family and his God-given talent to hit a golf ball.

And that was why, after the excess of showbiz events culminating with the Morgan chat show, he stepped out of the limelight. Time to go back to work. Now he concerned himself solely with preparations for The Open at Royal St George's. It was rumoured that he would arrive at Sandwich in Kent on the Tuesday afternoon and, as in Bethesda, would complete two long practice rounds on his own. The plan would be for nine holes on the Tuesday and another nine on the Wednesday, with the idea of 'there being no point in fiddling with a winning formula'.

Rory also admitted that he would love for The Open to be staged in his native Northern Ireland at Royal Portush Golf Club in Portrush, Co. Antrim. The last time the tournament was held in Ireland was in 1951 at Portrush, when Englishman Max Faulkner triumphed. However, Arlene Foster, the Tourism Minister for Northern Ireland, told the *Daily Mirror* that she 'believes the course could be ready to stage a major event as early as 2016.'

Indeed, Rory was all for it being held at Portrush: 'to have an Open Championship in Northern Ireland would be incredible. It has been a long time since it's been here – I think the course is definitely good enough.'

And there was another fillip for Rory as he counted down the days to St George's: after his win in the US Open, he was elevated to No. 3 in the world rankings. It was cause for further celebration in the McIlroy household and in UK golf generally as for the first time in the 25-year history of the rankings, Brits held the top three spots.

Rory had started the year at No. 10 in the rankings and gradually moved up to No. 4 yet the week after Congressional, he overtook PGA Championship winner Martin Kaymer, even though the German played in a further tournament and he didn't! Kaymer dropped to No. 4 after a poor display at the BMW International Open, which meant Luke Donald was ranked No. 1, with Lee Westwood at 2 and Rory at 3.

'We've fed off each other's success,' a beaming Rory told Sky Sports. 'We saw Lee get to No. 1 in the world and Luke has been very consistent for the last two years. We're working hard to beat one another and strive to be better than everyone else.'

But lifelong golfing fan Mark Paul was in no doubt that Rory was the real No. 1. He said: 'I have been a huge McIlroy fan for a while now. With Phil Mickelson ageing and Tiger Woods unable to find his health or his stroke, McIlroy looked like a young golfer with star power ready to go. He had performed strong at recent Majors, but fell short. But his US Open performance marked his official arrival. It was only going to be a matter of time before he claimed the top spot in the rankings. Only the maths is in the way of McIlroy earning that spot. I have nothing against Donald and Westwood, but I can't imagine anyone thinking that one of the two is the best golfer in the world – that title belongs to McIlroy, even if the rankings don't show it.'

Rory had made it clear that he would not compete in another event until The Open, but Donald and Westwood were preparing to take part in the Scottish Open while Kaymer was heading for the French. After the top four came three Americans: No. 5 Steve Stricker, No. 6 Phil Mickelson and No. 7 Matt Kuchar. Completing the Top 10 were Rory's fellow Ulsterman Graeme McDowell and Aussie Jason Day.

Rory's 2011 was shaping up to be an amazing year – he was rising in the rankings, he had earned more than £1.5 million in winnings and was ready to dazzle at The Open. At the same time, he was honest enough to admit that he still feared Tiger Woods, should the legend ever return to the form that once terrorised his rivals. It would be some match-up, should that happen. In the meantime, Rory also admitted he planned to make hay while Woods battled to recover from a leg injury.

Rory said: 'It's a good time for me to win things when he's not playing his best. The first thing for Tiger is to get healthy and see what happens from there. I don't know if anyone can answer if he'll get back to where he was 10 years ago, but a lot of people would like to see him back on the course.

'To have these 10 days off [after the US Open] is very nice – now I can try to win The Open. A lot of things go into winning a tournament. Obviously there's preparation and needing to play well – and you need a bit of luck. But I feel as if I'm playing well and have a really good chance of winning, and that's all you can ask for.'

He might have turned his attention towards preparing for The Open but the cash carousel that his US Open win had set into motion was speeding up, with an ever-growing band of individuals eager to seize their piece of the action. One enterprising company had even come up with the idea of combining Rory's attempt to win The Open in Kent with a luxury day trip on the Orient Express – for a fee of £360 for one of the rounds! The organisers set about enticing punters with a breathless promise of unbridled luxury in their blurb: 'Rory McIlroy became the youngest US Open champion since 1923 last week, breaking a host of scoring records in the process. Golf fans have the chance to watch him in action first-hand in less than a month as he sets his sights on the British Open Golf Championship at Royal St George's.

'McIlroy shot to the forefront of everyone's minds recently after his eight-stroke record win at the US Open on Sunday 19th June. He is now tipped as favourite to win the British Open Golf Championship over Tiger Woods. The 22-year-old sports star has also risen in the odds to win the BBC's Sports Personality of the Year in December.

'Golfing fans who want to watch McIlroy in action can combine the British Open Championships on 14th–17th July 2011 with a luxury journey on the Orient Express. The oldest and arguably the most prestigious of golf's four Majors, the Championship is being held at the Royal St

George's in Kent for the first time since 2003. Packages on the Orient Express from London Victoria to this remote location cost from only £299 per person (plus VAT) and are available on both Friday 15th and Sunday 17th July. Guests will enjoy a three-course Bellini brunch, a three-course dinner with wine, coffee, transfers, admission tickets, an individual course guide and VIP hostess assistance.'

Probably not a bad outing, if you add the spare cash – Rory à la VIP!

His success was also proving a real shot in the arm for his homeland's economy. Northern Ireland's Tourism Minister Arlene Foster said there was an 'international interest' in the Province as a result of his US Open win.

Speaking at the launch of the PGA EuroPro Open tournament at the end of June, the Minister announced: 'The recent success of current US Open Champion Rory McIlroy, and of Graeme McDowell before him, has generated a global interest in Northern Ireland and on our golf offering here.

'The PGA EuroPro Open tournament represents a unique opportunity to gain further widespread exposure. As well as highlights screened in the UK and Republic of Ireland, the tour will be broadcast in over 50 countries, including Germany, Asia and America. Holding high-profile golf events such as this will be crucial in further strengthening Northern Ireland's position as a world-class golf tourism destination.'

The 2011 event was to be held at Galgorm Castle Golf Course and Ms Foster added: 'The visitors that come to watch these events and the financial benefit they bring are of vital importance in stimulating growth and delivering economic value to many sectors of the local economy.

'Promoting our golf offering to an international audience and capitalising on the current global interest in Northern Ireland golf will help grow tourism here to a £1bn industry by the end of the decade.'

Back in Holywood, Rory's home was becoming a sightseeing target for groups of Americans eager to lap up McIlroy fever, according to *Daily Mirror* writer Oliver Holt: 'American tourists have started arriving, the girls in the local coffee shop are wearing golf gear and Holywood Golf Club has lowered its charge for a round to £16 in honour of Rory finishing on 16-under at Congressional. Nice touch.'

And the manager of one hotel and golf resort was similarly overjoyed by the business spin-offs his US Open win could generate. Rory is the touring professional at County Fermanagh's luxurious Lough Erne resort and its general manager, Jonathan Stapleton, revealed how business had dramatically picked up after an unwelcome quiet period – that there was 'huge interest' from guests who hoped to meet Rory there during their holidays.

'The immediate reaction has been extremely positive,' he told the *Irish Independent*. 'Rory is a very special young man and what he has done is quite incredible and is a huge boost for tourism in Northern Ireland. It was amazing to see it [the resort's logo] feature on the front page of most papers in the world. We are all very happy for him and his family. He is Northern Ireland's greatest ambassador.'

Rory was said to own a house at the resort and Mr Stapleton revealed that his parents, too often visit. He added that Rory was 'a very nice young man' who was 'only too happy to sign autographs.'

Northern Ireland's senior politicians at the country's Assembly were just as keen to get in on the act – pledging to hold a special reception for Rory to pat him on the back for his success in Bethesda. Business at the legislature was even suspended to allow all parties to praise him.

The Democratic Unionist Party's Peter Weir, who represents the North Down constituency where the family live, said the win marked Rory out as a 'true sports superstar.' Sinn Fein's Conor Murphy observed: 'I think it's a great tribute to him, as a very humble, a very grounded young man. It's a tribute to his parents and the people who have supported him, particularly in Holywood and the golf club there.'

And Ulster Unionist Leslie Cree added, 'This is, apart from a personal triumph, a great victory for tourism in Northern Ireland. He is going to be a great ambassador for sport and a great ambassador for tourism.'

Meanwhile, the SDLP's Karen McKevitt said: 'Well, we have got our own Tiger [Woods]. Our Celtic Tiger! He sold the brand of Northern Ireland so well – it was the way he did it. Yes, it was brilliant golf, but in a very modest way. He was spectacular, yet calm.'

Then a tale emerged that put into sharp focus just what a nice guy Rory was – how he could indeed lay claim to being 'the People's Champion'. After winning at

Congressional, he had gone off to make a charity appearance at Willowbend Country Club in Mashpee, Massachusetts. But instead of playing the big star by riding in a limo with his father Gerry and the US Open trophy, Rory travelled as a passenger with the local cop, who originated from Ireland and had been designated to give him a police escort on the 90-minute journey to Logan airport for his flight back home.

'He was absolutely a normal guy,' Barney Murphy, travelling with his Dutch Shepherd police dog Jaxx, told the *Boston Globe*'s Brian McGrory, 'He asked if he could ride in the cruiser – he said he really liked dogs. You know he's not going to become anything but a normal guy because he's so down-to-earth.

'He said he'd never been in a police car before and wondered if it would be OK. The whole country was screaming and shouting the day before, and there he is, sitting with me in the car. He was humble and courteous, not one bit of arrogance…'

Rory was already proving himself to be an extremely likeable, approachable champion, but soon he would have to focus on more serious 'business matters' as The Open loomed. On Wednesday, 29 June, he finally ended speculation about his build-up for the tournament in outlining a plan of attack. He revealed how he did indeed plan to be the last man of the 156-strong field out at St George's, saying: 'I will spend two days at Sandwich on the Thursday and Friday of next week. I'll then stay away until the Tuesday afternoon when I have a press conference but I won't play until the Wednesday. It's good to arrive there fresh because there's so much going on at a Major.'

It was suggested to him at a press conference that he had perhaps been taking things too lightly by having a three-week competitive break before St George's – and getting involved in a long list of celebrity events. He laughed it off, replying, 'I've been on the range and am spending Thursday and Friday with my coach, Michael Bannon. I'll ensure I've prepared properly.'

He also said that he would continue to take note of Nicklaus's comments that he needed to harden up, mentally and emotionally. The former champion's words of advice had worked wonders at Congressional after that collapse at The Masters – and Rory was determined that he would build on the emotional structure, even if this led to some people accusing him of 'turning nasty'. At an earlier promotional event for his clothing sponsor Oakley, he had said: 'There definitely is that sense when you win a Major, people are going to see you and come at you a little different. And honestly, there is also a difference in the way you approach it yourself. You do have that kind of superiority complex in a way and I don't think that is a bad thing at all. It takes a while to figure it out and understand things and get perspective, but yes, a superiority complex can be a positive. You have to get yourself into this mentality where you think you are going to go out there and beat everybody else.'

He told Yahoo! Sports that he had been more arrogant when he was younger, but had made a decision to change because he didn't like what he had become. The only problem then was that he became 'too nice'! 'The thing with me is that I was very cocky as a kid. When I was growing up, I was winning all these junior tournaments. Then, when I got older, I realised that is not a nice way to be and not the way I wanted to come across. So, I toned it down a lot and I went a bit too far the other way. I think I got to the point where I was almost being a bit too nice.

'You have to force yourself to be a bit arrogant in a way, and that is not something that comes totally naturally to me, but it is something that can be of benefit. I was a bit too conscious of how I was coming across. Inside I have that bit of swagger and belief in my game and I need that on the course. Now I have found a good balance.

'When I was winning as a kid, it made me feel like I was better than everyone else. When you love golf so much and it is so important to you, doing well at it gives you this sense of self-importance. The way I view things now is very different. I may be better than you or most people at golf, and I can say that and feel that and it doesn't matter because I am. Facts show that.

'But there are a million and one things that other people are much, much better than me at, and those things are just as important. So, that keeps it in perspective a bit. I feel now that I should have perhaps won more considering some of the golf I have played. Winning is what it is all about.'

Indeed it is. And while Woods was rapidly beginning to look like yesterday's man, Rory continued to notch up the volume with each new success. Ten days after the US Open win, however, Tiger finally broke cover to comment on his new rival – and to warn that he was not finished yet. Speaking to the media back home in America, he admitted to being mightily impressed by Rory's showing at Congressional. Tiger said: 'That was pretty good, wasn't it? That was some seriously good playing. It was cool to see that he had softer conditions and he was able to go low, but also was able to continue pushing it. And that's what's fun when you have a lead, is to keep building on it and keep pushing. Those conditions weren't such where pars were going to build leads and an occasional birdie.

'You had to go out there and be aggressive, and go get the birdies because everyone else was; everyone else was making three, four, five, six birdies a day, and he just didn't make any bogeys. That was very impressive playing. To do that at a US Open, to be that aggressive the entire time, that was cool to watch.'

Tiger even conceded that Rory was a better player than he had been at 22 – a comparison originally made by Woods' good friend Mark O'Meara: 'I totally agree with what Mark said. In comparison to, well, in '97 when I was, what, 21, granted, I had some success but I didn't like my golf swing. That's why I changed it. I felt like at the same age, yeah, his swing is definitely better than mine was at the same age.

'But in '99, my swing came together and I had a pretty good next two years. That's kind of where we're at the same age comparatively, yeah, his swing is better. He needs to obviously continue working on it and continue getting better.'

But it was then that the Tiger roared, dismissing those who

claimed he was about to be usurped by his new young rival. 'I'm 35, I'm not 65,' he declared. 'I've still got some years ahead of me! Golf is unlike any other sport. I mean, Watson was, what, 59 years old when he almost won? We can play for a very long time. And given that we have the health to do it, guys have succeeded for a very long time.

'That's what I would like to do is play this game for as long as I want to. I feel like my best years are still ahead of me.'

Those words sounded ominous but one voice firmly behind the belief that Rory would soon usurp Woods was American amateur Scott Pinckney, who had played a practice round with him the day before the real action started at Congressional. After his feats in the tournament itself, Pinckney told Reuters that Rory's form was 'ridiculous', adding, 'He hit it great in practice, as you can tell from what he's done in this tournament. And then he got to 13-under (par) during the second round. It's awesome.'

Pinckney was in no doubt that Rory would now go on to take the No. 1 spot, eclipsing Woods in the process. The American said: 'He definitely can – he's got the talent and he's got the mindset. There's nothing but up for him and soon he will reach the top.'

Indeed, the unpalatable fact of the matter for those who still believed Woods would make a comeback worthy of Lazarus was this: Tiger hadn't won a title for almost two years as Rory tuned up for his assault on St George's (the Australian Masters in November 2009). And as the Irish youngster zoomed up to No. 3, Woods languished at No. 17, his lowest ranking since 1997. If Rory could now go on to win The Open, if he could sort out his mindset and physical fitness, the statement of intent to his hero and biggest rival would be crystal-clear: You've had your time, this is mine.

CHAPTER 16

A BRIT
OF ALRIGHT

While many of those around him and in the press box started to panic, Rory stayed cool and calm. That was the situation surrounding him as the build-up to The Open at St George's intensified. After the near-hysteria and massive hype that followed his triumph at Congressional, the usual British characteristic of knocking a man down after building him up began to surface.

Some pundits also urged caution on the grounds that he could indeed be Tiger Woods Mark 2 – in the sense that Woods went 10 Majors without winning after his 12-stroke triumph at The Masters, back in 1997. Would Rory now fall victim to a similar curse – especially as he was taking it so easy when, the critics argued, he should have been out taking part in tournaments in between the US Open and The Open – or at least practising hard?

There was talk in the press boxes and on the public debating sites that Rory may indeed have blundered by not spending enough time getting his mindset and his strokes, too, in shape for the tournament; that he had been too busy having a good time, that he should have practised more instead of taking three weeks off before what many considered the world's biggest Major.

He himself was wise enough to know he might face some flak for taking time out, however. To that end, he got his defence in first before the three-week hiatus, saying: 'With success comes expectation – I know expectations on me are pretty high now but I expect big things of myself, anyway. As long as I keep committed and dedicated, I don't see any reason why I won't handle it well. I always wanted to believe that I could win a Major. I feel if I can keep this form up, I have a good chance at the next two Majors.'

Of course, it was not as if our boy had been out on the town every night until the early hours. No, he had merely taken the decision to step off the carousel and unwind a little after the crazy days of The Masters and the US Open. He had, quite sensibly, decided to ease off the pedal slightly – to come down off the golfing high and rest a little and play a little. In his spare time, he was also doing a few secret practice rounds – in the backyard of his home in County Down! He had built a mini-golf course on land at the back of the house but this was no poor man's show – no, it had cost him hundreds of thousands of pounds and boasted four greens plus a rough with sand, all kept in tip-top condition by his very own greenkeeper.

Indeed, Rory felt no guilt about his time away from the

game and was not at all fazed when Piers Morgan asked him about it on the broadcaster's *Tonight* show on CNN. In fact, he took the opportunity to explain exactly why he believed this could be of major benefit to him: 'Time off and time away from the game is nearly as important as the time you practise because if I play golf every day, you get stale, you go through the motions, it becomes a little bit tedious. But once you go away from the game for a couple of weeks, you get that freshness back, that determination and hunger that makes you want to practice.'

It made sense and an American psychoanalyst friend of mine confirmed as much. Roz Hoskie said: 'I don't know what all the big fuss is about. The guy seems pretty easy-going and clued up anyway, so he probably knows himself what is best for him. I watched him in The Masters and in the US Open and he seemed to be in control at both. I know he let it slip at The Masters, but that doesn't mean he had a breakdown or anything like that. It just means he veered off his normal course a little at that particular time. It can happen to anyone at any time – even the coolest of characters. You just lose a little concentration or your mood dips a little and there you go!

'His performance at the US Open proved it was merely a little wobble at The Masters and that he had settled back into his normal implacable routine. As far as him taking three weeks off after winning – well, that would seem the move of a genuinely intelligent guy to me. Someone who has a clear vision of what it takes to stay focused; someone who knows that it makes big sense to just step away from the field for a while and draw breath. After all, he had pretty much been in the limelight without a break for two months. Good on the lad for doing what he thought was what – I think he made the right call.'

That was my belief, too, at the time, although many pundits and hacks were determined to make a big thing of it. One told me: 'Just you wait and see – the proof will be in the pudding if he flops big-time at Sandwich. Then he'll maybe wish he *had* committed to another tournament or two instead of swanning around with a load of bloody celebs!'

After Congressional most golfing pros were generous in their praise and their belief that Rory would now go on to dominate the game. Colin Montgomerie, however, broke rank as he prepared for the Scottish Open to voice his opinion that the youngster might have been better served 'fitting in a tournament or two' before The Open – rather than taking such a long break. Monty said: 'I can understand having two out of three weeks off, but I would like to have seen Rory play a competitive tournament between the two Majors.

'Rory's so natural, I don't think there are any fears about his game but it's the locker room – there will be so many people wanting to congratulate him, wanting to talk to him. That's bloody tiring. Whether it was the French or the Scottish Open he could have got that out of his system, so he could start The Open afresh. Now he's got all that ahead of him and by the time he gets to the first tee, I think he will be mentally tired. But who am I to say?'

And it wasn't too long before some other fellow pros now started to urge caution when discussing Rory's potential. Paul McGinley and Darren Clarke were first to break from the pack with fearful voices, suggesting it was perhaps time to dampen the level of expectation on Rory at the British Open.

Speaking at the French Open, Dubliner McGinley said: 'Rory's a great talent and a smashing kid to boot but some of the hype's just way over the top. Give the kid a break! He's won three tournaments. One is a Major, which he won in Rolls-Royce style, yet his career is a long way from where it could be considered anywhere near Tiger's. It's just very premature to be placing that expectation on him and no one knows that more than Rory.'

Clarke had known Rory for 13 years and had taken the week off during the BMW International to celebrate with him. He said: 'It was a pleasant and unexpected week off, but it was all for a good reason. But I'm not sure we should be labelling Rory the next Tiger or Jack. All we know is that he's just won his first Major in unbelievable fashion. That Rory's got masses of talent is obvious and judging by the way he's handled himself so far, he'll be well able to cope.

'So, I'm sure Rory will want to win many more Majors. Hopefully everybody's expectations won't burden him too much. Rory has good managers around him, while his parents are very smart – they'll ensure he keeps his feet firmly on the ground. I know one thing, he doesn't need my advice!'

Meanwhile, the journos and writers were also on Rory's case, basically claiming he had become too big for his boots. Their argument was summed up by golf blogger Travis Houser, who commented: 'The newly coated US Open champion Rory McIlroy is still gloating in his Major victory

10 days after winning the tournament. Taking last weekend and the next two weekends to promote his sponsorships rather than play another golf tournament since he wants to soak in his last victory due to it being kind of a big deal.

'Rory McIlroy won a big deal tournament, now he is stating he wants to be known as a big deal. Hearing a golfer say that he is going to force himself to be more arrogant is not a wise thing to be saying when he is coming off one of the biggest choke performances, in which he cried on the 13th hole at The Masters, in golf's past decade. Rory wants to 'force [himself]' to be arrogant since it is 'not naturally' him because he sees that other superstar athletes use it to strive for their own dominance in their sport.

'Rory McIlroy's next tournament will be the British Open. Strangely, the same tournament in which his dad waged his buddies arrogantly that Rory will win before 2014.'

But there was one voice determined to be heard above the din of pessimism enveloping Rory as The Open loomed ever closer – Justin Rose, who had finished fourth at the event when just 17 and an amateur in 1998. Rose was unstinting in his praise and in his belief that, yes, Rory was strong enough to handle the growing burden of expectation placed on his young shoulders: 'What a great start for a 22-year-old to notch a Major under his belt that early. I don't feel sorry for Rory having to bear that burden of expectation now. He's earned it, he deserves it: he's a great player!

'He plays golf with a great attitude. I think the way he handled Augusta was probably as impressive as his win, to be honest – the way he bounced back from that.'

Rose added that Rory had inspired him and given him hope that he too could now get out of a rut that threatened to derail his season: he had earned no Top 10 finishes since March and had missed three cuts as he set about defending his ATT National crown at the start of July 2011.

Rory also earned a salute from his counterpart on the female tour. While he himself had won the US Open at 22, Yani Tseng won the LPGA Championship shortly afterwards at the same age – and her 10-stroke romp in the LPGA was as impressive as his. It meant that she had become the youngest woman ever to secure four Majors. The Taiwanese player sent her congratulations to Rory on his 'brilliant achievement' but when asked what the secret of her success was simply smiled and said, 'I always have a great time out there on the green! I try to stay as relaxed as I can.' It was certainly a powerful message – from a real winner – to those who claimed Rory was wrong to relax before The Open.

Tseng also admitted she felt a 'connection' with Rory, having known him for some years on the greens: both had played in the same invitational juniors event run by Nick Faldo. She explained to Reuters: 'I think it's like four girls and four boys from Europe, United States and I'm from Asia. Because I won a junior tournament, you get to play in the Faldo Series. You have training for like, two weeks over there and Nick Faldo came the last three days to play with us and give us a little advice. I was in Palm Springs for two weeks but I don't speak any English, so it was very tough for me.

'Rory was there. I wish I could speak better English and I could talk to him more. I think I was 13 or 14. Very young.'

Tseng was certainly blazing a trail that left even Rory in her slipstream as she underlined her dominance of the women's tour in clinching the LPGA Championship in New York with a record-equalling low score. She had closed with a 6-under 66 to win by 10 strokes, finishing at 19-under 269 at Locust Hill Country Club. Her triumph at the tender age of 22 meant she had stolen the record previously held by Se Ri Pak, who was 24 when she won her fourth Major. It was also Tseng's eighth career LPGA Tour victory, her second in a row and third of the season. Rory would have to keep winning big, if he was ever to catch up with her!

And a British newspaper editor Simon Kelner, then editor of the *Independent*, added his voice to those 'celebs' who had met Rory since his win at Congressional and been bowled over by his charm. In awestruck tones, this giant of the UK media industry wrote: 'Editors can be very blasé. This is particularly the case with ones who have been around a while, like yours truly. (I know what you're thinking: how does he manage to look so young? You're not? Oh, well…) Anyway, we lead extremely privileged lives, and we get to meet many influential, inspiring and interesting people. In my time, I have sat next to Bill Clinton at lunch and had the very moving experience of meeting Nelson Mandela. I have seen the inside of No. 10 on more than one occasion, and have even had the honour of being cold-shouldered by the Duke of Edinburgh. So I hope you understand that I'm not being fancy when I say that my bar is quite high when it comes to being impressed.

'In that context, I can't fully convey what a thrill it was to meet the golfer Rory McIlroy this week – meeting him was a pleasure way beyond the opportunity to pass on some awestruck congratulations. He was charming, modest and level headed. In an era when sporting heroes increasingly are shown to have feet of clay, here is a young man from Northern Ireland who you feel will know how to handle the success that undoubtedly lies ahead of him. Oh, and thanks for having your picture taken with me.'

It was a fine tribute from a well-respected veteran of the newspaper world.

But now, as if to stress he was keeping one eye on the day job – and that he planned to embark on a busy schedule again – Rory interrupted his three weeks off to let it be known that he would take part in the 2012 Honda Classic. He committed early to the event – in which he had competed for the previous two years – through his agent, Chubby Chandler, at the same time as did Lee Westwood. 'Lee and Rory both like to play the Honda Classic,' said Chandler. 'I am not sure whether it's the golf course or the fact that it is in between two World Championship events and the guys go over for three straight weeks. And West Palm Beach isn't the worst place to hang out for a week. So I've already committed Lee and Rory to next year's Honda Classic.'

He also put Rory's name down for the Hong Kong Open scheduled for December 2011, saying it was one of his 'favourite tournaments.' The previous year, Rory had finished 6th there and said he planned to improve on that: 'It will be very special to be announced on the first tee as the US Open Champion. Hopefully I can bring some of that Congressional form to Hong Kong and give the fans a great show. It is such an amazing city with a very special energy and every time I go there, I just love the place.'

One thing regarding the ever-looming Open was becoming clear: it was highly unlikely that Rory would come up against the Tiger at St George's. In surely the right move, Woods looked set on a course of convalescence to heal his injuries. Many pundits argued this was the only way he would ever be able to take Rory on and win, if he were back to full-strength. Oliver Brown best summed up Tiger's predicament, writing in the *Daily Telegraph*: '"I have played in pain before," Woods said. "I have played injured, and I have played through it. I have been very successful at it. A number of years, I have been hurt more than people could possibly understand – and I have won." He can no longer pull that trick in the Rory McIlroy era. Thanks to the US Open champion's remorseless front-running at Congressional – remind you of anyone? – the paradigm has shifted. Unless Woods takes the requisite steps to complete his convalescence, he risks being rendered a ceremonial golfer, kicked into the long grass by the young buck chasing his records. Mercifully, he is pre-empting such an outcome, saying: "I won't come back just to show up. I'm coming back to win."'

English golfer Ian Poulter even came out in public to urge Tiger not to show up at St George's – arguing that he should recuperate and he could still return to battle with Rory at the very top of the sport. Poulter, now ranked at world No.

14 and above Woods for the first time in his career, told the *Daily Mirror*: 'He won't play and he probably shouldn't play. To be honest all he needs to do is get himself fit. If he comes back too early, he is going to be back out of the game for a while. He has been so good for golf that I think everybody would like to see him fit, healthy and where he can just play with no injuries.

'If that means he has to take the rest of the year off, if that were me, I would be taking the rest of the year off. I don't think he should pressurise himself and I am sure he won't – he will come back when he's ready. But when he is back, he will be a factor. Tiger was comfortably twice as good as anyone else when he got to 20 points in the world rankings. A half Tiger would still compete to be World No. 1.'

It was then revealed what the prize money would be at St George's. We have already noted from Rory's father Gerry that he wasn't obsessed about money but he must have been pleased that The Open was at least keeping pace with the cash on offer with the Majors held in the States. The winner of The Open would get £900,000 – an increase of £50,000 on the previous year – to bring it into line with the other three Majors. And the overall prize money had also risen: from £4.8 million to £5 million.

The bookies gave Rory another boost or, if you viewed it another way, added to the weight of expectation in making him early 6:1 favourite to win the event. Lee Westwood was second favourite at 10:1 with Luke Donald winging in at 15:1.

Rory earned another fillip when he received confirmation that his star was indeed rising — and fast — in America. He was told he had been named the American nation's top rising sports star to watch in July 2011. To achieve that distinction, he had had to overcome some major US sporting names including runner-up, pitcher Johnny Cueto of the Cincinnati Reds, and catch king Tony Gwynn Jnr of the Los Angeles Dodgers, who was 3rd.

The awards were handed out by Brand Affinity Technologies (BAT) — a company in the States that calculates daily consumer likes and dislikes based on a combination of media exposure, performance, awards, popularity, engagement and fan base among 45,000 athletes and celebrities.

This accolade proved that Rory had already made a big name for himself in the US and how he was, even at the age of 22, well on the way towards establishing himself as a household name over there. That ever-growing fame was then bolstered as several American golf bloggers and writers admitted they were not as concentrated on the AT&T National event at the end of June/beginning of July because of the massive shadow Rory had cast over the sport.

Paul Foeller best summed up the situation when he wrote on the US fans' website Sports Central: 'I'm sitting here, still two weeks before the British Open, focusing almost none of my attention on either Tiger or the field that's competing in the AT&T National. Instead, I'm eagerly waiting to see what Rory McIlroy will do in the British Open. For the first time in a long time, somebody without the last name Woods has single-handedly made golf exciting again – and made it worth talking about before Sundays.

'A game that is often called a gentlemen's game finally has a leading athlete that actually exhibits the class and demeanor of an at least loosely defined gentlemen. So let's not pretend, like some naysayers, that McIlroy can't be as important to the sport as Tiger was because he's not good enough. Even if he wasn't good enough to eventually be that dominant (and he is, by the way) that's not the only reason he matters to golf. It's a combination of that skill and his aforementioned composure, both on and off the course, that make it plainly obvious just how big a deal Rory McIlroy can be when all is said and done.'

But it wasn't just the bloggers and writers who were so taken by Rory's exploits. No, even the Republican Party were keen to praise him – and offer him up as an example of how they could beat Barack Obama in the 2012 presidential elections! Republican strategist Matthew Dowd told the US press that Rory was inspirational and that his party could learn from him: 'Before Rory McIlroy's triumph fades in our memories, it's worth considering the lessons the young Irishman's US Open victory offers for the 2012 presidential race. As he headed into the US Open weekend, McIlroy explained that his strategy was to set an overall goal, do his best, play things out in small segments on the course (in his mind, three holes or so at a time), and not pay much attention to the leaderboard. This strategy served him well since he was able to hold The Open trophy after setting tournament scoring records. His approach could be a model for Republicans who want to take on President Obama in the 2012 general election. Setting a goal and then playing it out day by day is also great advice for living our lives.'

Dowd added: 'Take the race in small segments as McIlroy did, and know that doing well in those segments adds up to achieving the overall goal. The nomination process for Republicans will be determined by many factors but the election candidate who approaches the contest as McIlroy did is likely to end up playing in the final twosome in the fall of 2012 against President Obama. In the process, the election candidates should stay grounded and not take themselves too seriously. As McIlroy's mom reportedly said to him over and over again growing up, and as I heard in my Irish household many, many times: "Get over yourself".'

It was a quite remarkable example of how young Rory McIlroy from Holywood, Northern Ireland, had made the world sit up and take note. A promising young golfer (and his mum!) were now being held up as examples of how to do things right and how to win by America's electoral gurus.

What next? The invitation to the White House by an Obama determined to use Rory's popularity to help him get re-elected? Certainly, I would not bet against it.

Back home in Ireland, Padraig Harrington bigged up his young mate Rory, urging the crowds to come out at St George's to witness history in seeing him play. He said: 'Anyone who is interested in golf has to see this great talent at 22, so that you have something to compare him with when he is winning Majors galore. He is a talent worth seeing now. He's right on top of his game but he could go forward from here and be one of the all-time greats.

'You want to be one of the people who can say to your friends, "I saw him when he was 22." I would certainly want to come and watch Rory right now. A lot of other professional golfers will want to as well.'

Harrington also told the *Daily Star*'s Cathal Dervan that Rory himself should ensure he savours the occasion. He added: 'Rory has to enjoy it. He should walk around with the swagger of a young man and soak up every minute of it. Everybody is going to want to see him and he has to enjoy it, really enjoy it. He has to enjoy the experience of being US Open champion and accept that people will genuinely want to see him and welcome him because of what he has achieved.

'He can really enjoy his success at the US Open over the coming weeks. Regardless of what he does this month, it is a very special feeling to be holding a Major trophy and playing in a big tournament. He should enjoy that experience. It doesn't come around all that often so he should make an effort to really draw on it from the crowds. It is an experience he will never forget.'

The veteran star signed off with a quote that will surely go down in the history books of 20 years' time when Rory has won many more Majors, coming up with this classic line: 'Rory could be a player like we have never seen before. He has the ability to transcend golf, to bring people into our sport who would never have thought of golf before – and that should be applauded.'

In the first week of July 2011, that growing prominence within the game – and ability – highlighted by Harrington was reflected in Rory winning the European Tour's Golfer of the Month for June in recognition of his eight-shot US Open victory. The young Irishman felt honoured, but was still cheeky enough to quip: 'I hope this will not be the last Golfer of the Month award I receive after winning a Major championship!'

At the same time, Lee Westwood appeared with a plea for Britain to now build on the newfound level of success and popularity nurtured by players such as himself and Rory. He argued public funding to host more golfing tournaments was needed if it were to continue, telling Press Association Sport: 'The strength of British golf is amazing at the moment. We all watch Wimbledon clinging on to the one British hope in tennis, yet in golf, you can look down the world rankings and see so many people who could win a Major. That shows you the kind of talent we have in this country at the moment.

'Nick Faldo asked 10 years ago – when I was the only one in the Top 100 of the rankings – where the next one of me was coming from. Now I think we have got a few people who could win multiple Majors. I think if you can't take advantage of the quality of golfers we have at the moment, then when are you going to do it? It is a shame to let that just pass by. Finances are tight at the moment but when you look at how much the Spanish government have invested in golf – they have seven [events a year] in Spain this year, France has two or three and England – the hotbed of golf – has one. I am not sure why there is only one.

'With so few opportunities some people are going to miss out. When I came on tour, we were playing four or five tournaments in England. We need lots of opportunities because we are not short of facilities.'

It was a fair point and certainly one worth bearing in mind as the euphoria over Rory's feats continued to hog the headlines. Indeed, he even threatened to overshadow the men's finalists at Wimbledon on Sunday, 3 July when he earned a standing ovation and many affectionate looks from the women (and men!) present at Centre Court before settling down to watch Rafa Nadal and Novak Djokovic do battle. The *Independent*'s James Lawton summed up the scene in a few amusing lines: 'If Rory McIlroy had any doubts about his impact on the nation's imagination they surely dissolved on his visit to Wimbledon last week. Holy cow, as my esteemed colleague Nick Bollettieri might say, he commanded almost as much attention as Pippa Middleton.

'He did it for two major reasons. One was because he is young and wonderfully optimistic and thus far at least blessedly unmolested by the onset of celebrity. The other was that no casual visitor to SW19 was more entitled to breathe the air so filled with excellence.'

Lawton also called for Tiger Woods to rise up like Lazarus to face Rory at The Open, but Woods was slowly recovering from his injuries – and staying out of the limelight, as he tried to rebuild his battered image. He had re-emerged to praise Rory for his triumph at Bethesda and to reveal that he still faced a daily battle to keep his demons at bay. He told reporters: 'I need to be a better man going forward than I was before. And just because I've gone through treatment, doesn't mean it stops. I'm trying as hard as I possibly can each and every day to get my life better and better and stronger, and if I win championships along the way, so be it.'

They were positive words and gave hope that finally the former legend who could previously do no wrong had learned from his mistakes; that he could now move forward and start to pick up the pieces of his shattered life and career. And no one would have liked that more than Rory McIlroy: the young Irishman had once worshipped Woods and eagerly learned from him on courses around the world. After winning the US Open, Rory would famously say: 'I'm not playing for money – I'm playing for a place in history.' While that line summed up everything good about the boy and his ambitions, it also pointed to the fact that he actually needed Woods to return one day in top form otherwise certain burnt-out, pessimistic old hacks and analysts would inevitably say Rory had only succeeded because of Tiger's demise. That he wouldn't have achieved it had Woods – who was still only 35 when Rory triumphed at Congressional – been around and firing on all cylinders.

To achieve that indisputable place in history he so coveted, Rory needed a top-form Tiger around to prove he could beat him but he would have to wait at least until after The Open. Surely Tiger would not gamble with his injuries only to end up beaten and demoralised?

CHAPTER 17

A NEW SUPERSTAR

Tiger Woods would eventually end the 'would he/wouldn't he make The Open' debate by officially withdrawing from the tournament on 5 July 2011, a week before it got underway at St George's in Sandwich, Kent. The former World No.1, who had been out of action since mid-May with a leg problem, finally conceded defeat in his race against time to be fit for the event. He said: 'Unfortunately, I've been advised that I should not play in the British Open.'

It would be the second Open he had missed in four years – the three-time champion was also missing at Royal Birkdale of 2008 following reconstructive knee surgery straight after his US Open victory, a month earlier. Woods added: 'As I stated at the AT&T National, I am only going to come back when I'm 100 per cent ready; I do not want to risk further injury. That's different for me but I'm being smarter this time. I'm very disappointed and want to express my regrets to the British Open fans.'

But it didn't change things as far as the punters were concerned – Rory had always been favourite, had Tiger made it. That he didn't manage to do so made no difference to the odds, as Betfair revealed: 'Woods was matched at a low of 5.7 to win at Royal St George's, but had drifted out to around 27.0 before the announcement was made.

'Given the drift and his anticipated withdrawal, the market has not moved a huge amount since the announcement – Betfair customers unwavering in their belief that Rory McIlroy should go off clear favourite for glory.

'The US Open champion trades at 7.2 to win the third major of the year – far clear of English rivals Lee Westwood (12.5) and Luke Donald (19.0). Questions have been raised over McIlroy's preparation by Colin Montgomerie and Padraig Harrington, who have both criticised the US Open champion's three-week layoff since winning at Congressional. Montgomerie and Harrington believe the attention McIlroy will receive could tire the 22-year-old before he reaches the first tee. "When you've won and you go to your next tournament, there are 155 other players and 155 other caddies who want to say well done," said Harrington.'

Phil Mickelson also pinpointed Rory as the favourite to lift his first Open, saying: 'He has got the ability to turn it on and shoot low scores. He did that at The Masters and at

The Open last year, with 63. And to come out and win the US Open a month ago with some very impressive play, everyone has got to look at what he shoots because he is a threat every week.'

A couple of days prior to the event getting underway two £20,000 bets were wagered on Rory to win The Open. The pressure on the boy was intense but he batted it away with his usual easy-going attitude. In fact, he explained this was one of the reasons why he had taken so much time off before the tournament: to escape the constant limelight.

Rory was all smiles, however, as he arrived at the pre-tournament press conference, making it clear he was glad to be in Kent and that he felt refreshed and was raring to go. He said: 'First and foremost, I'm very happy to be back at The Open. It's obviously a tournament I look forward to every year. The first 10 days after winning the US Open it was a bit hectic, trying to see everyone and going here, there and everywhere, but the last 10 days has been good. I've got back into my routine, been practising a lot. I was here last week for a couple of days and got two good practice rounds in, so I feel as if my preparation has been really good coming in here. It was nice to relax and sort of take it all in after the US Open but I knew that the time for reflection wasn't really at this point of the season, it's at the end. I've got to forget about what happened three weeks ago and just come in here and try to win another golf tournament.'

He then defended himself for taking almost a month off, saying: 'I was scheduled to play in the French Open but if I had played it, I knew I wouldn't be giving the best of myself or been able to practise or prepare properly. Every event I go into, I want to have a chance to win. I knew my preparation wouldn't have been good enough going into France to have a chance. So I thought, you know what, let's just get everything out of the way and make sure that your preparation going into The Open is as good as it could be and that's really what I've done. For me it's all about preparation. I went into The Masters after three weeks off and shot three pretty good scores there so it's not a problem to me not playing competitive golf after having a break.'

He admitted he had been surprised by the reaction to his win at Bethesda. 'I didn't realise how much of a fuss it would create or how much of a buzz,' he said. 'It's been nice. I thought it was great for me to win the US Open, win my first Major, and the support that I've had from people back home, from everyone from all over the world, has been pretty overwhelming. It's a very nice feeling to have that support walking onto the golf course.'

When asked how he planned to play St George's, and how his approach would differ from Congressional, he answered: 'It's a completely different golf course – it's firm, it's fast. But the thing is, with this wind you're going to have to keep the ball low. But sometimes it's hard to run the ball into these greens because they're so undulating and they can go so many different ways. I think you're going to really need a very strong ball flight, especially if the wind still picks up. I don't think you'll be able to run many shots in because, as I said, it can catch the wrong side of a slope and it can go 20, 30 yards away from the green.

'I played last week on Tuesday and it was basically flat calm. There were a few drivers and then on the Wednesday it was pretty windy, so I got to see the course in two different conditions, which was pretty good. I think this golf course is going to be all about the second shot and making sure that you get the ball in the right position on the green – because the greens are so slopey you're going to have 25-, 30-footers all day if you do hit them.'

Soon the time for talk was over, it was time for action – and the outcome? Well, I hate to admit it, after previously backing Rory's stance, but maybe some of the pundits who argued that he had taken too long out of the game were right – or at least half right. Yes, he looked rusty and out of sorts as he stumbled through a tournament that he should probably have dominated, struggling in tough weather conditions, failing to get totally to grips with the course and to battle for a Top 10 spot, let alone take on his old mucker Darren Clarke, who would go on to lift the claret jug. Like Rory in Bethesda, Clarke would prove an immensely popular winner at Sandwich.

Rory got an inkling that it wouldn't be all plain sailing when he went round in a one-over-par 71 on the first round – which left him six shots behind leader Thomas Bjorn of Denmark. He got off to a stinker, bogeying two of the first three holes but then pulled his game together, making just one bogey and two birdies the rest of the way. 'I felt after the start that playing the last 15 in one-under was a pretty good effort,' he would later say. 'It was a day where you just needed to grind out a score – anywhere around even par was a good start. I holed a couple of nice putts for par and yeah, it was a day where you just needed to grind out a score. Anywhere around even par was a good start.

'On a day like this, I know better than most people you can shoot a high number and put yourself out of a golf tournament so it was nice to go out and shoot a decent score. I said yesterday if the conditions stayed the same, I'd take two 70s over the first two days and if I shoot 69 tomorrow with similar conditions, I'll be really happy going into the weekend.'

But did he believe that he would be among the contenders on the back nine on the final round? 'Yeah, definitely,' he insisted. 'I don't feel as if I have to do that much differently – I just need to keep it tight, keep it on the fairway, hit a few greens and just take birdies here and there because I think that's going to be the key this week, to keep it around even par.'

It had been noted that Rory was showing more patience in recent tournaments and benefiting from the approach. Had this been deliberate? 'Yeah, definitely, but that comes from experience. Every time I play a Major or I play an important event or get myself into contention, it's just a great experience for me heading into the future. It was a great experience last year at St Andrews, shooting 80 in the second round – I learned a lot from it. And it's building that experience up and learning from your mistakes, that's been the biggest improvement for me this year.'

Rory upped his game on the second day, carding a 69 that left him just four shots off new leaders Darren Clarke and

American Lucas Glover, with US PGA champ Martin Kaymer and overnight joint leader Thomas Bjorn among a four-strong group a shot behind. He was naturally delighted for his former mentor Clarke, 42, saying, 'It's brilliant. This sort of golf really suits his game – he's grown up on links and he likes to play different shots. It's the sort of week where you've got to just manage your game very well and he's good at doing that, hitting different shots and changing the trajectory. It's good to see him up there. He's doing a bit better than me at the moment, but I'm planning on changing that.'

Meanwhile, Rory admitted that his own round had been 'a grind' and the course was tough-going: 'It was a grind. Even though it was sunny and looked nice out there, it was very tricky. The course is playing a lot firmer, a lot of crosswinds, and to shoot something in the 60s today I'm very pleased with. It would have been nicer to be a couple better, but I'll take that going into the weekend. I'm very happy with my position and within striking distance of the leaders.

'Everything is working pretty well. It's just a matter, as I said yesterday, of keeping it tight and not hitting too many loose shots and keeping it around par because with the weather coming in tomorrow, something around that score is going to be very close. It's the same for everyone and there's only seven shots separating this field; it's very open.

'I think you'll see a lot of chopping and changing at the top of the leaderboard, but it's the most open Open I've seen in a long time. I think it'll be exciting to be a part of, and it'll be exciting to watch over the next two days.'

It would be exciting to watch and play in – but not for Rory as he bombed during the final two days at Sandwich. His only consolation would be watching lifelong pal Clarke win his first Major. Rory would shoot a disappointing 74 in the third round at Sandwich, a total that, realistically, meant he would have to wait at least another year – and Lytham – to scoop his first Open in Britain.

Once again, he would blame the bad weather. A year previously he had blown it at St Andrews with that 80 in the wind and rain, now he would follow up with the 74 – in the wind and rain. But it was pointed out that his 4-over-par card was actually nearly a stroke and a half below the field average (75.412) despite a double bogey-7 at the 14th hole when he hit his tee shot out of bounds.

'You've got half of Kent on your left and you hit it right, it was a bit disappointing,' he would say of his tee shot at the 14th hole. 'When the weather is that bad, you seem to lose a little bit of your rhythm or a little bit of your timing. And when the weather is like that, if your timing is off a little bit, it can magnify the misses.'

He was nine strokes off the pace and knew it would take a miracle for him to go on and overwhelm Clarke, who was now setting a pace he would never relinquish. Rory being Rory he refused – in public, at least – to throw in the towel, however. 'What did Paul Lawrie come back from? Ten shots?' he asked at the post-round press conference, a reference to the Scot's final-day recovery at Carnoustie in 1999. 'Well, it's been done before, so I'll just have to keep the hope. If the conditions are decent, I could see myself going out and shooting maybe 4- or 5-under, and getting in the hunt. If the conditions are similar to what they were this morning, then it's going to be very tough.'

And the forecast? More rain and wind...

Rory spoke a little more about his day's exploits (or lack of them), adding: 'It seems in this tournament, you need to get a good draw and it just hasn't really worked out for me this week. It was really tough out there this morning and I felt for the first 13 holes to get through those in 2-over-par was a pretty decent effort. And then to give two shots away on 14 was very disappointing. I tried to make a couple of birdies coming down the last four holes, but wasn't able to do it and I think 74 was the best I could manage.'

It was suggested he lost a bit of self-belief at the 14th. 'Yeah, I mean, you've done so well for 13 holes to keep yourself in it and then it was a tough one to take. It's a big setback. I obviously wanted to go out and get myself closer to the lead and not further away from it; I wasn't able to do that today. I'll need a good one tomorrow, and if it doesn't look like I can win, I'll try my best to get a Top 10 or a Top 5.'

At least he was upbeat at seeing Clarke edge ever closer to his first Major. 'Yeah, it's fantastic! He birdied the 1st hole today, which was good. He's waited a long time to win that Major and it would be great if this week was the week where he could get his first one.'

Clarke shot a one-under 69 to take a one-stroke lead into the final round and to put Northern Ireland in position to claim its third Major championship in a little over a year. 'If somebody had given me 69 before I was going out to play, I would have bitten their hand off for it,' he conceded. 'We did get very fortunate with the draw. Sometimes to win any tournament the draw can make a big difference but in The Open Championship, it makes a huge difference. We got very lucky.'

And he knew there was a lot of work still to do. He stood at 5-under 205, with Dustin Johnson just one shot behind after his second straight 68. And Rickie Fowler, also with a 68, was on 208, tied with first-round leader Thomas Bjorn. While Clarke would now go on to triumph, Rory was to curse the weather and his own bad luck: he would finish with a 73 for a plus-seven total of 287. That would leave him tied for 25th – a disappointing outcome after he had arrived at Sandwich with high hopes of glory.

In comparison Clarke would win the tournament with a 5-under total of 275, three shots clear of Phil Mickelson and Dustin Johnson, who tied for runner-up. Bjorn was 4th on 279.

The *Daily Mail* best summed up the nature of Rory's loss at Sandwich: 'As the wind and rain swirled across the Kent coastline on Saturday, Rory McIlroy's hopes of a double Open triumph were blown away like a sailor in distress. In contrast to the gloriously sunny temperatures in the mid-eighties at Congressional – where the 22-year-old Ulsterman played near-flawless golf to win the US Open and anointing as the new superstar of his sport – McIlroy was confronted with some of the worst weather an English summer can conjure and slid out of contention at the 140th Open Championship.'

Rory did not try to disguise his disappointment at the outcome but again made it clear he felt the bad weather had played its part: 'It's been a tough week for me. I felt like I did well the first couple of rounds and I just struggled a bit in the bad weather at the weekend. I'm not a fan of golf tournaments where the outcome is predicted so much by the weather – it's not my sort of golf. I'm disappointed with the way I finished obviously, but I'll just have to wait until next year to try and make a good run at this tournament.

'I'm looking forward to getting back to America, playing in Akron, and playing in some nice conditions. Obviously the PGA and the Irish Open is a big one for us as well – it's a week that I enjoy.'

Had he come to Sandwich with the right attitude; that he would win even if the weather happened to be bad? 'Yeah, of course – all I was trying to think about was winning this tournament. There's no point in coming in thinking I'm the US Open champion, I'm going to do well – you can't really think like that.'

The pertinent point, that he might have to get to grips with the bad weather if he were to one day win The Open, was put to him: 'Yeah, it's either that or just wait for a year when the weather is nice. No, I mean, my game is suited for basically every golf course and most conditions but these conditions I just don't enjoy playing in, really – that's the bottom line. I'd rather play when it's 80 degrees and sunny, and not much wind.

'Obviously Clarke is so good in this weather that it's not surprising to see him up there. Mickelson is playing great. He's played a lot of these Opens and tried to adapt his game to it, so there's a little bit of experience that comes into it.

'I obviously have high expectations myself and I know if the weather had have been a little better this week, I probably would have been able to contend a bit more but it's just the way it goes. All the amateur tournaments I've won were played on links courses, but they were all relatively calm so I just play better and my game is more suited to calm conditions. Just glad I'm in the clubhouse, I'm just glad I'm in!'

So, would he now take another break before the Irish Open – or would he practise more? 'Hopefully, if the weather is decent at home, I'm going to spend a few days getting my swing back to where it needs to be. The wind messes it up a little bit, so I'll work for two or three days just working on it and getting it back into a nice groove. Then I'll take it easy and head to the Irish Open next week, or the week after.'

He then added that he would now be leaving his press conference and heading for the clubhouse, where he was determined to lift his spirits by cheering Clarke on to that first Major. His final quotes of the tournament were to stress exactly what a win by Clarkey would mean for Northern Ireland, as well as he himself: 'It'll be a very emotional victory for a lot of people. He's had to go through a lot of things and it's almost as – especially back home in Northern Ireland – he's the forgotten man a little bit, with Graeme doing what he did last year and then me coming on. So it would be fantastic to see him win, it would be great.

'He's been fantastic [to me]. He's been a great friend. He always sends me texts when he's not playing, he sent me texts all week at the US Open and he's been a great help. Anything I've needed or wanted to know, he's always been on the other end of the phone, which has been a great help for me.'

It would now prove Rory's major consolation in a weekend in Kent that had promised so much and delivered so little. As his friend roared to the victory he so richly deserved, he clapped and cheered him on. To add to his three previous rounds of 68, 68 and 69, Clarke closed with an even par 70 to lift the claret jug for the first time. For the previous 10 years, he hadn't contended in a Major, hadn't even been eligible for the last three Majors and was no longer listed in the world's Top 100, but just as Rory's win at Congressional had proved so popular with the masses so now would Clarke's. The man himself had an explanation as he gave an interview with the claret jug by his side: 'I'm a bit of a normal bloke, aren't I? I like to go to the pub and have a pint, fly home, buy everybody a drink, just normal. There's not many airs and graces about me – I was a little bit more difficult to deal with in my earlier years and I've mellowed some, just a little bit, but I'm just a normal guy playing golf, having a bit of fun.'

Steven Howard, chief sports writer on the *Sun*, best caught the spirit of Clarke's victory: 'There can rarely have been an Open triumph quite as popular as this one. Well, perhaps if Tom Watson had sunk THAT putt at Turnberry two years ago. This, though, was one to cherish and one that will be remembered for a lifetime by all those at Royal St George's yesterday.

'Darren Clarke, Open champion. How does that sound? Probably the best-received victory since the late, great Seve Ballesteros, who died earlier this year, won at Lytham in 1988. One that was roared along by a gallery who still couldn't quite believe it even as it became more and more likely.

'And one that was firmly linked to Seve when, just before Clarke finally got his hands on the claret jug, there was a long and heartfelt round of applause from a packed 18th-green crowd for the triple Open winner. And all under a fluttering Spanish flag.

'The embraces for Clarke from rivals Phil Mickelson, Thomas Bjorn and Miguel Angel Jiménez also showed the huge regard in which the Ulsterman, a special member of the golfing fraternity, is held.'

As Clarke won the tournament, Rory tweeted: 'Northern Ireland. Golf capital of the world!!' Clarke was told about it and, even in his moment of supreme glory, found generous words for Rory, the young man he had helped to become a potential golfing great. 'We're blessed to have two fantastic players in Rory and G-Mac,' Darren said, 'and I've just come along, the only guy coming along behind them. We have fantastic golf courses, we have fantastic facilities, but to have three Major champions from a little, small place in a short period of time, it's just incredible!'

Of course, there was much analysis and a good deal of toing and fro-ing about why Rory had messed up at Sandwich when he had been expected to stroll to victory. My view remains that he simply does not like the bad weather, that it hinders his progress. It is a failing and one he will surely have to deal with by spending more time practising in those very conditions that drive him to despair (and make him drive to despair). Otherwise he would seem a natural candidate to become a more active member of the PGA Tour, where the weather is normally certainly more to his liking – and where he often seems to produce his best golf.

Yet one other possible reason for his blow-up would emerge in the days following the tournament. For it was revealed that he had split from his long-term girlfriend Holly Sweeney, one of the constant, steadying influences on his life, before The Open. A statement released by his management team on the Monday after the tournament confirmed the two were no longer an item: 'Rory McIlroy's long-term relationship with Holly Sweeney came to an amicable end before the British Open,' it said.

Then, just days later, it emerged that Rory was now dating the world's top tennis player, Caroline Wozniacki of Denmark, who at 21, was a year younger than him. The *Daily Mail* reported: '[They] fell for each other after they were seated together to watch David Haye and Wladimir Klitschko in Germany on July 2. The pair were clearly infatuated with one another from the start, as they began publicly flirting on Twitter.

'When Rory's management confirmed his "amicable" split from Holly last week, he embarked on a new romance on the final day of the British Open. The night before she tweeted him to wish him luck in the tournament. After their original meeting, Caroline wrote on Twitter: "Fantastic fight! Also met Rory McIlroy, who was sitting just behind me :) Really down to earth great guy :)" He responded with birthday wishes on July 11, joking: "You're getting old." She suggested he could buy her a legal drink in the US now she was 21.'

My opinion is this was all media tittle-tattle and Rory was far too professional to let his private life infringe on his golf – he just had a bad week at Sandwich, fuelled by the poor weather conditions which he was at least honest enough to admit he detests any time, anywhere. But some golfing fans felt he had taken his eye off the ball with Caroline. One summed up the general feeling that, like any young man, he could be distracted if he didn't keep his concentration 100 per cent on the game at which he excelled: 'Rory McIlroy should stick to practising with his golf bats rather than running around after girlies and attending boxing matches. He is a good golfer but doesn't need to be distracted.' Another said simply: 'Rory, forget about the tweeting and concentrate on your golf!'

In essence, the gossip was irrelevant. As I say, I am convinced it did not – and never would – impinge upon his game. But the interest served one useful purpose in epitomising just how far the young, hopeful, dreamy boy from Northern Ireland had come. No longer simply the property of Ireland, he had become headline news across the globe. His every move was about to be analysed and dissected by a press and public hungry to learn every minute detail about the life of the youngster who had pushed golf back onto the front and back pages for all the right reasons after the very public humiliation and downfall of its former golden boy, Tiger Woods.

Some would continue to say Rory McIlroy had rescued golf at a time when the sport badly needed a saviour and in so doing, he had relinquished his own privacy and become one of the most famous sportsmen in the world.

We were now entering the era of Rory McIlroy, superstar.

CHAPTER 18

ON TOP OF
THE WORLD

At the start of January 2013, Rory McIlroy sealed what the BBC would call 'the most lucrative endorsement deal in British sport' from Nike. It was estimated that Rory, now 23, was in line for a cash bonanza that would send his head spinning. The boy-next-door from Holywood, Northern Ireland, would earn up to $250million (£156m) over five years.

The BBC's Tom Fordyce summed it up like this: 'If accurate, those estimates mean McIlroy's deal is substantially bigger than both Tiger Woods's most recent 10-year Nike contract – reportedly worth £124m – and David Beckham's lifetime deal with rivals Adidas, estimated to earn the footballer £100m.'

Nike Golf president Cindy Davis explained why they had

laid out such a staggering amount. She said, 'Rory is an extraordinary athlete who creates enormous excitement with his on-course performance while, at the same time, connecting with fans everywhere.

'He is the epitome of a Nike athlete, and he is joining our team during the most exciting time in Nike Golf's history. We are looking forward to partnering with him to take his remarkable career to the next level.'

And Rory said, 'I chose Nike for a number of reasons. They are committed to being the best, as am I. Signing with Nike is another step towards living out my dream.'

Some cynical pundits suggested there and then that his dream appeared to have changed shape – that the dollar signs had become more important than the winning of tournaments. That Rory's head had been turned by the fame, the women (he was still with tennis superstar girlfriend Caroline Wozniacki) and the big-time lifestyle. That he had forgotten his roots and was now embarking on the very lifestyle he had once dismissed as not for him, when he had said, 'For me it's not about the money. I have always dreamt of playing golf simply to win big tournaments.'

So had he really changed for the worse – or was it simply a case of envy and jealousy from the press corps who had documented his rise from nobody to the very pinnacle of the golfing world? My own feeling is that it was probably a bit of both: that, yes, he had engaged energetically with a more opulent lifestyle and that, yes, it was typical of the press reaction in most sports when the man or woman they made hits the top…the build-'em-up and knock-'em-down syndrome.

But is there any 23-year-old guy who wouldn't be left a little breathless if a wad of notes was flung at him? Sure, Rory's life did change, but it was heading that way anyway – he was the world's No 1 golfer and it would have been a strange thing if his environment and the people within it had not altered to reflect his phenomenal progress.

As we explained in previous chapters, as Rory moved on up the ladder, so did his life. By the end of 2011 even, he had changed management and girlfriends and had bought himself a nice luxury house. He wore expensive clothes and a watch to match. Within another 12 months, he had put his home in Northern Ireland on the market as he admitted for the first time that he was spending more and more time in America.

The lad from Northern Ireland liked the warm weather on the other side of the Pond and it made sense for him to base himself in the States – as he was away from his native land for 50 weeks a year, playing international tournaments. He said he particularly loved Florida – and it would be in the so-called 'Sunshine State' that he would set up home in his new life.

Rory had put the Northern Ireland pad on the market – a mansion in 14 acres – for £2million and said, 'I have really enjoyed living here. It is a really special place which has allowed me to relax and unwind – when I get time!'

His new home in Florida was even more special. It had six bedrooms – as opposed to the four at his former home in County Down – cost almost £7million, and also boasted nine bathrooms! 'It meant he could go and use a different bathroom each day of the week!' a source close to the McIlroy camp joked. 'He had hit the big time and was splashing money about like there was no tomorrow, as if it didn't matter – which it probably didn't given the amounts he was now earning.'

The house – in Palm Beach Gardens – also had its own swimming pool, gym and a jetty from which Rory could launch a motor boat. Indeed, a fan of Rory's in Belfast, quipped, 'The next item Rory will be purchasing will no doubt be a yacht to go alongside his jetty.'

And, as if to confirm his new-found status as a major celebrity sportsman, Rory's home was just down the road from another golfing ace…Tiger Woods. But if he were to remain Tiger's No 1 rival on the golf course – as well as off it as the dollars rolled in – Rory would need to maintain his form on the golf course. Rory's ascension to the World No 1 spot had coincided with Woods seemingly being in decline. But as 2011 turned into 2012, the Tiger had started to regain some of his old swagger and form. Rory would need to be at his best if he were to keep his biggest rival at bay, but just as Tiger improved, Rory seemed to struggle. There was more talk that things off-course were affecting his game. That he wasn't concentrating enough on his golf; that his celebrity status and the money were going to his head.

As 2011 became 2012, he urgently needed to claim another major – to silence the doubters and to maintain his position as Woods's main rival for that world No 1 spot. The back end of 2011 had summed up Rory's year: brilliant at times, so disappointing at too many others. He had blown his last chance of 2011 to secure another major – when he flopped at the PGA Championship at Atlanta Athletic Club in August. It followed on, of course, from a similar disappointment in the Open a month earlier.

Rory suffered a strained tendon on his right wrist on the 3rd hole of the first round after attempting to play a shot from behind a tree. To his credit, he played on but never really looked to be in contention. Rory finished the event in tied 64th after carding an 11-over total of 291. Afterwards he commented, 'To be honest I'm glad to be done. It was a struggle. I basically played 70 holes of this tournament not at 100 per cent, so it was always going to be tough. Still, I made some good play out there in the last few days and birdied the last.

'Now I'm just looking forward to a couple of weeks off, and you know, get rested up and get ready for the end of the season.'

It would be a more successful time for Rory in that 'end of season' period. He won the Shanghai Masters after a tense playoff against Anthony Kim at the end of October 2011. The victory also brought him a winner's purse of $2million (£1.25million) – the richest prize in golf. It was the third playoff of Rory's career and his first event since dropping Chubby Chandler as his manager for Horizon. Afterwards, Rory said, 'I've been close in two or three tournaments and had two thirds and two seconds and was finally able to get myself over the line today. This was the third play-off of my career, and I was able to win this one, so at least my record in these events is getting better. I am just delighted to get another win.'

A couple of weeks later he finished tied for 4th at HSBC Champions but, more importantly, moved up to world No 2 in the rankings, at the time his highest ever ranking. And in December 2011, he rounded off a pivotal year in his career development in style by triumphing in the Hong Kong Open by two strokes with a closing round of 65. Rory sank five birdies in a bogey-free final round at the Hong Kong Golf Club to record a final score of 12 under par and finish two shots clear of playing partner Gregory Havret.

Rory admitted the win meant 'something special' to him. He said, 'I've loved this city, this golf course, this tournament ever since my first Hong Kong Open in 2007. I felt like it owed me something after the playoff in 2008. I had to wait a few years for it to finally happen – but to get my hands on this trophy now and to win this tournament is very special.

'No matter how prestigious tournaments are, you always have your favourite, and this is definitely one of my favourite tournaments and to be able to win it is fantastic. I couldn't be happier.'

It had certainly been some year, what with his first major win at the US Open, after the earlier disappointment of the Masters blow-up, and the subsequent ones in the Open and the PGA. To end 2011 on a high meant a lot to Rory – and now he was determined to go out and add a second major to his bow in 2012.

But it would not be easy – just as landing that first major at the US Open had taken hard graft and emotional ups and downs after he had lost his mojo at the Masters. In his first tournament of 2012 he would show his encouraging form from the end of 2011 was continuing as he finished runner-up in a strong field at the Abu Dhabi HSBC Golf Championship. Up against the likes of Tiger Woods, Luke Donald and Lee Westwood, Rory ended up just a single stroke behind eventual winner Robert Rock, from England.

Rory was pleased with the outcome, saying, 'It's a good start to the year. It's nice to go out there in the final round of the first tournament you play with a chance to win. I could have maybe made a few more of the opportunities that I presented myself, but I played solid enough out there.'

It was the second year in a row he had finished second in the event, and he summed it all up by saying 'it was something good to build on' for 2012.

Indeed it was, and by March, Rory was roaring as he won the Honda Classic, a win that propelled him to the ranking of world No 1 for the first time. It was all the sweeter as he held off a determined, on-form Woods to lift the trophy. Woods hit a 62, the lowest final round of his career to heap the pressure on Rory. But the wunderkind coped admirably to maintain his place at the top of the leaderboard.

The tournament's own press department swiftly pushed out a release summing up Rory's achievements, 'He poured in the 8-foot birdie putt on the 13th for a two-shot lead. He gouged out a wedge from grass so deep he could barely see the ball to save par on the 14th, and he twice saved par from the bunker on the scary par 3s for a 1-under 69 and a two-shot win.

'[By doing so] McIlroy became the 16th player to be No 1 since the world ranking began in 1986, and the fourth player in the last 16 months since Woods abdicated the top spot after a five-year reign. McIlroy replaced Luke Donald and became the second-youngest player to be No 1 behind Woods, who was 21 when he first got to the top after the 1997 U.S. Open.

'Additionally, McIlroy moves into the top five in the FedExCup standings for the first time in his young career, checking in at No 4.'

Rory was hitting form as the 2012 season began to shape up and he celebrated his win by flying to New York to spend time with his girlfriend, Caroline Wozniacki. Before he jetted off, he outlined what the win meant to him and how he hoped it would now lead to greater things. He said, 'It was always a dream of mine to become the world No 1 and the best player in the world or whatever you want to call it. But I didn't know what I would be able to get here this quickly. Hopefully, I can hold on to it for a little longer.'

Three-time major winner Padraig Harrington had no doubts that Rory was now here to stay at the top of the rankings. He paid tribute to the youngster, saying, 'There's very few players as good at him at his age out there winning tournaments. There are guys with potential, but he's already delivered. And he has a good balance in his life. He doesn't look like a guy who is going to burn out. He looks like he's going to be here for a while.'

The Masters was just a month away and the press corps and the public were, inevitably, wondering how he was feeling about his return to Augusta after his very public blow-up the previous year. Presumably the win in the Honda Classic would lift his spirits and help him overcome any nerves or fears that he might suffer a similar meltdown this time round? Would he be changing anything in his preparations? Rory answered confidently, saying, 'To be honest I'm approaching it similar to last year. I'm taking three weeks off before the Masters to prepare. I'll go up to Augusta the week before and play a couple of practice rounds, and if I can do the exact same thing this year as I did last year for 63 holes, I'll be doing OK. So hopefully I can do that again, and if I could get myself in that position, maybe finish it off a little better like I did at the Honda today.'

But his run-in to the Masters went off course in the next two tournaments. He finished third in the Cadillac Championship in Miami, two strokes behind Justin Rose and was gutted when Luke Donald took the world No 1 title back off him after his friend won the Transitions Championship. Donald finished his final round at Innisbruck in Florida with a 5-under 66 and then triumphed in a four-man playoff against Jim Furyk, Robert Garrigus and Sang-Moon Bae.

Donald was delighted to have won back the No 1 spot after a couple of weeks. It was his fifth win in his last 31 events – and it meant he would stay at the top of the pile until the Masters at Augusta. Rory was down but honourable enough to tweet his congratulations to Donald. 'Well I enjoyed it while it lasted! Congrats @LukeDonald! Impressive performance!' he said on Twitter.

Donald was just as gracious, saying, 'I'm sure he got a taste of the view and I'm sure he'll want more of it. He's a great player. I think golf is in a good spot right now. There's a lot of excitement going on.'

That excitement would ramp up several notches as Rory and the cream of the world's golfers now descended upon Augusta for the 2012 Masters. The big question on everyone's lips was: Could Rory set out a similarly scorching pace as the previous year, but finish it this time?

The answer would be a despondent 'No' as Rory struggled to make his presence felt. He went into the weekend just one stroke off the lead but found the last two rounds difficult – and that is putting it mildly – as he eventually finished in a tie for 40th. It was not his finest hour and the UK papers were united in their criticism. Some even accused him of 'choking' as he had done the previous year when he appeared in an unassailable position.

The *Sun* led the way. 'Rory McIlroy suffered yet another Masters meltdown in a flurry of shocking shots in round three. McIlroy wilted under the pressure a day earlier than last year, when his final-round 80 saw him throw away a four-shot lead. A triple bogey at the 10th was the flash-point for an awful back nine of 43 a year ago,' the paper reported.

'This time he imploded on the front nine, opening with a double bogey as he played them in 42 – six over par. McIlroy again cut a forlorn figure as he kept leaking away shots, throwing in another double bogey at the seventh hole, sandwiched by bogeys at five and eight. So after setting out just a shot off the lead, McIlroy found himself consigned to the also-rans, one over for the tournament and a horrifying five over for the day.'

A visibly deflated Rory said afterwards, 'It was a disappointing weekend, just one of those things. I played pretty well over the first couple days and then just came out on Saturday and really didn't get it right in that front nine, and that killed me for the rest of the tournament. But I'll come back next year and try my best again.'

It was turning into a topsy-turvy season of highs and lows as Rory tried to keep up his momentum when he had it, and not let the disappointments weight too heavily upon him. But it was proving a most difficult balancing act as the campaign progressed. For instance, after the Masters letdown he regained the world No 1 ranking in the middle of April – but lost it again to Donald at the end of the same month.

Then, in the first tournament of May 2012, the Wells Fargo Championship, Rory finished a creditable runner-up to Rickie Fowler – which meant he once again returned to the summit of the world rankings. Inexplicably, though, Rory then went on to miss the cut in his next three tournaments – the Players Championship in Florida, the PGA Championship at Wentworth and the Memorial Tournament in Ohio – which, of course, would once again cost him the No 1 spot.

One of the lowest points of the campaign came in June when Rory failed to make the cut at the US Open, the event that had propelled him into legend when he had won it – and his first major – a year previously. The *Telegraph* neatly summed up his anguish with the headline – 'Rory

McIlroy's latest cut is the deepest of all'. And BBC Sport put it all into its full grim perspective, 'Defending champion Rory McIlroy…missed the cut at the US Open after failing to recover from a poor first round. World number two McIlroy missed out by two shots after carding a three-over-par 73 to finish 10 over. McIlroy struggled from the outset in San Francisco and carded 77 in round one. McIlroy won by eight shots and broke a host of scoring records when he finished on 16 under at a rain-softened Congressional 12 months ago but the 23-year-old was unable to cope with the firmer, faster conditions of Olympic's Lake Course.'

Afterwards, Rory admitted he was 'obviously disappointed'. He said, 'It wasn't the way I wanted to play. I left myself with a lot of work to do after yesterday's round, and to overall I don't feel like I played that badly for the last two days.

'It's just such a demanding golf course and just punishes the slight test shot that's off line or that's maybe not the right distance or whatever and that's how I feel. You really have to be so precise out there – if you're not, you're going to get punished. We're just not used to playing this sort of golf course week-in, week-out.

'We're not used to having to land balls before the edge of the greens to let them run on. It's just something that you have to adjust to in this tournament. I wasn't able to do that very well this week. It hasn't been the greatest run over the last six weeks, or whatever it is, but I still see enough good stuff in the rounds that gives me hope that I'm not very far away.'

Hope, Rory may have had – but that certainly did not translate into drastically improved finishes as he struggled to get back to the level of excellence he had achieved at the US Open in 2011. When the Open at Lytham came around in July 2012, there was renewed optimism that Rory might finally put it all together at once. But again, there was only disappointment as he finished tied for 60th, finishing with a dismal eight over par.

Rory said, 'My game wasn't there. It was pretty good on the first day but after that I struggled and couldn't find anything. I'm obviously disappointed. It is hard to make up shots on this golf course. I felt coming into the tournament I was playing pretty well, but when you try to force it and press things trying to get momentum, it just doesn't work.'

Rory denied that he had a mental hang-up about the Open – or that his constant underperformances in the event were because he felt it was the hardest to win. He said, 'I feel like I can win in any given week if I play well. I think they're all equal. I don't think there's any major that's harder to win than another. You've just got to beat the other guys that are playing. I treat them all equally and just try and do the best I can.'

His fans were beginning to despair of him ever recapturing his best form, but Rory is a battler and he put in extra hours on the tee practising and streamlining his strokes as he attempted to put things right. He told his close friends that he believed he was on the way to winning again – and that he still believed he would triumph at another major soon.

If he were to do that in 2012, he would have to be quick.

The final major of the year was pencilled in to start just a couple of weeks after his poor showing at the Open in Lytham. Rory revved up for the US PGA by finishing tied for fifth at the Bridgestone Invitational in Ohio.

He arrived at Kiawah Island visibly more confident than he had seemed for weeks and it showed in his work as he performed majestically in 2012's last major. Rory roared to victory, covering himself in glory and plaudits as, at last, he put the doubts and poor showings behind him to win the US PGA. The *Mail's* Derek Lawrenson superbly summed up Rory's achievement in the light of his previous ups and downs. 'The summer of learning for Rory McIlroy and the state of flux in the sport he plays have both come to an end in the most emphatic of ways,' he said.

'Four days was all it took to restore order to the world of chaos. Four days of ruthless brilliance from McIlroy and the conversation has shifted from 16 different winners of 16 different majors to how many one man can win in the years to come.

'One record-breaking win at the US PGA Championship on Sunday, and all foolish talk of Caroline Wozniacki being some sort of Yoko-like distraction (younger readers, ask your dad) has been thankfully buried.'

Rory achieved the vital win by finishing 67-66 to end 13 under on a tough course. He won the tournament by a record eight strokes – overwhelming the previous one held since 1980 by Jack Nicklaus, who triumphed by seven. The tearing up of the history books didn't end there – Rory had also become the youngest player to win two majors since

Seve Ballesteros won the 1980 Masters Tournament, and the sixth youngest of all time. The US PGA victory also helped him regain the coveted world No 1 ranking.

Nick Faldo was one of the first to offer his congratulations to Rory – and to outline how he believed the Irishman was heading for true golfing greatness. Faldo said, I think we saw at Kiawah, as we did at the US Open last year, that he is a very special golfer. I didn't win my first major until I was 30 and yet here he is at 23, with all that knowledge of winning already gained.

'The only other golfers in recent times to win two majors at his sort of age were Tiger, Jack and Seve and that's exactly where Rory should be ranked. He is that good.'

Before the event Rory had admitted 'taking his eye off the ball' during that lean spell that led to three consecutive failings to make the cut earlier in the year. Afterwards, he was a much relieved young man and said he was 'just glad it had all turned out right' after so many ups and downs and harsh criticisms he had experienced in 2012.

He said, 'I just had a good feeling about the week. Earlier in the summer I was frustrated with how I was playing but a few people pushed panic buttons for no reason and it did motivate me. I don't think I could have answered the criticism in a better way. To call myself a multiple major Champion…I feel very privileged to join such an elite list of names.

'And to win my second major and get to world No 1 all in the same day is very special.'

Very special indeed – and Rory would now go on to win three more tournaments before 2012 became 2013. He finished top of the leaderboard in the Deutsche Bank Championship, in Massachusetts, almost three weeks after the US PGA and also won the BMW Championship in Indiana at the start of September and was crowned the DP World Tour Championship in Dubai at the end of November.

In between those three triumphs, Rory would also play his part as Europe retained the Ryder Cup in Medina. The win was all the more satisfying as the Europeans had looked to be out of it as the final day of play dawned. Europe produced a brilliant comeback to win the trophy. The United States had needed just four-and-a-half points from the 12 available on the day, but Rory and Co grabbed a magnificent eight and a half of them to clinch victory from the jaws of what had seemed certain defeat in a 14½-13½ win. Rory saw off the challenge of the talented Keegan Bradley 2&1 as Europe won it on the final day.

Rory said the celebrations went on late into the night and told how he had enjoyed the comradeship. He said, 'To bring this group of guys together; to all play for the same cause; we win together, we lose together, and luckily the last two Ryder Cups, we have won together.

'I said this at the start of the week – there's nothing better than celebrating a win with your team-mates. We don't get to do it very often, and it's just so nice to have these guys around and to celebrate it with them.'

Of his own performance on the last day of play, Rory added, 'I was just happy to get a point to help the team. When I saw the match-up I liked it, I liked playing one of their strongest players.'

It had been a great second-half of the campaign in 2012 as Rory romped to those four individual wins and the triumph at the Ryder Cup. It was sometimes easy to forget that he was still only 23!

After a relaxing Christmas and New Year, Rory determined to win another major in 2013. But as this book went to the printers in May 2013, the plan hadn't materialised as Rory would have hoped. In four tournaments on the PGA Tour, he had won none and secured just one top ten finish – when he was runner-up in the Texas Open. In The Masters, he had ended up in a disappointing tie for 25th. He had also missed the cut in the European Tour's HSBC Championship in Abu Dhabi in the January.

And in February, 2013, Rory was lambasted when he withdrew from the Honda Classic, saying he had been suffering toothache. His critics had claimed that was not the problem, that the toothache was a smokescreen – and that he was actually struggling to make his mark with the new clubs he was now using.

Initially, Rory had defended his decision to withdraw, saying, 'This is one of my favourite tournaments of the year and I regret having to make the decision to withdraw, but it was one I had to make.'

But later he would concede that he had made a mistake walking off the green at the event. He said, 'I realised pretty quickly it was not the right thing to do. I regret what I did. It won't happen again. There is no excuse for quitting. No matter how bad I was playing, I should have stayed out there. I should have tried to shoot the best score possible even though it probably wasn't going to be good enough to make the cut.

'I have been struggling with my lower right wisdom tooth for over a year. So, yeah, my tooth was bothering me, but it wasn't bothering me enough to probably quit. But that's just the way it is.'

At least he had been big enough and honest enough to admit his error. He was one of sport's good guys and he would be back on track soon; of that he was certain. As 2013 progressed Rory McIlroy was determined to add to the two majors he had already clinched at such a tender age. No one doubted that he would do so – and that there would be many more over the years. He was still golf's No 1 at the age of 23 – and intended to stay there for years to come: Rory McIlroy was a legend in the making. No doubt about that.